DISCARDED

In Tribute to

Mrs. G. W. Hays

this book is given
Lamar State College of
Technology

Miss Crystal Canon

LIMESTONE and LOG

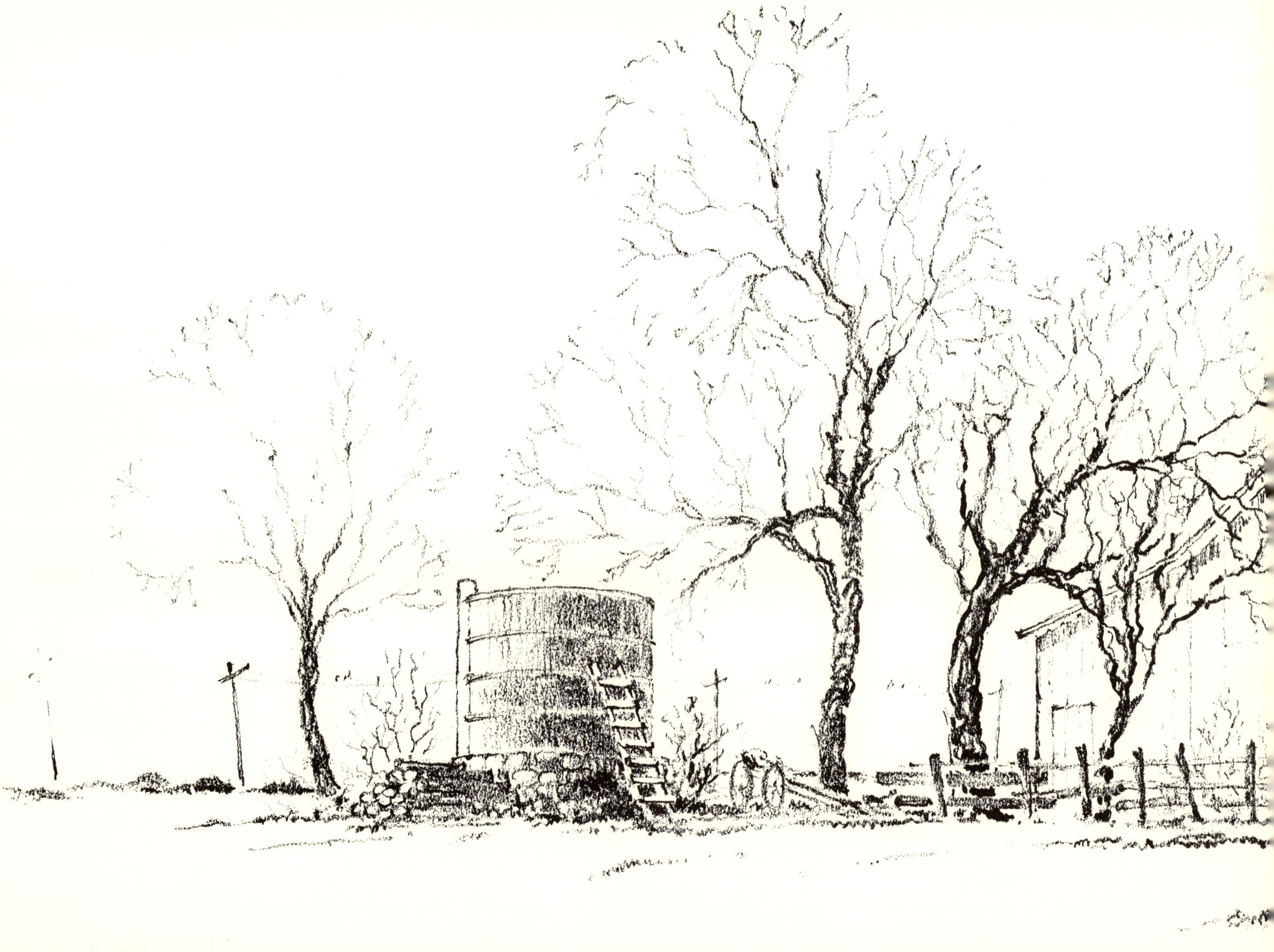

LIMESTONE and LOG, A HILL COUNTRY SKETCHBOOK

by J. ROY WHITE · *with text by* JOE B. FRANTZ · *Introduction by* HARRY H. RANSOM

THE ENCINO PRESS

© 1968 : THE ENCINO PRESS : 2003 SOUTH LAMAR : AUSTIN

For Mary

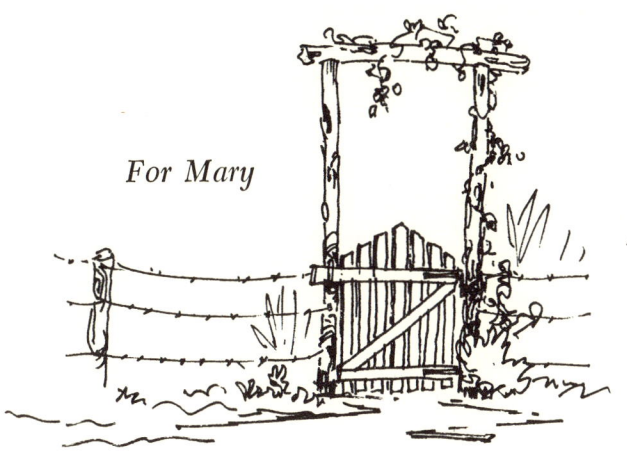

And dedicated to the Women
of the Hill Country
who have accepted the land
as they found it
and made of it a home.

INTRODUCTION

JOE FRANTZ, professor of History and director of Research in Texas History at the University of Texas, is more than a distinguished historian. A disciple of Walter Webb, Frantz has become an interpreter in many idioms and in the widest sense of Southwestern life. From distinguished accounts of business development to perceptive biographical sketches, from reflections on the cultural growth or incidental conflict in the state to sharp-eyed interpretation of the future, Frantz has proved himself a deft but courageous spokesman for both sensible and sensitive understanding of the region.

A graduate of the University of Texas School of Architecture and now a member of a firm of distinguished architects, Roy White is also an artist of delicate skill. A gentle man, he sees and captures the beauty of these early Texas dwellings, formed by men of the frontier of materials at hand and after the memories they brought to a new land of still earlier homes far away.

Roy White and Joe Frantz have captured and held for those who will come after them the charm, the pathos, and the still, quiet beauty of a vanishing time within the pages of this book.

HARRY RANSOM

The University of Texas
Austin, Texas
November 7, 1968

THE MOOD OF THE HILL COUNTRY

TO THE EAST the country falls away and flattens out into a watered valley and plain that stretches to the Gulf of Mexico and to the Mississippi Delta country. To the west the country seems to ravel out as it moves toward the sun. The grass grows thin and then ceases to grow at all. The trees stunt, and then disappear. Not even the ubiquitous and pesky cedar and mesquite can survive in quantity as the western country becomes higher and drier.

The sign on Highway 290 on the way west from Austin has just one entry: El Paso 594 miles. Beyond El Paso is Phoenix and beyond Phoenix is Los Angeles. These are the only three watering places for nearly 1500 miles that can imaginatively be called cities. Austin does grow a little toward the west and El Paso edges eastward, so that in the past decade the sign has seen its figure changed from 598 miles to its current low cipher. In this exploding population and concomitant sprawl, the distance between cities in this area may become negligible in another one or two thousand years.

So the sign implies that as you leave Austin, a combination state capital and oasis, you will encounter nothing for a long, long day's drive. The implication is almost correct, for the few place-names that slow you down are such household words as Fredericksburg, Junction, Sonora, Ozona, Fort Stockton, Balmorhea, and Van Horn. Anyone who can't drive from Austin to El Paso in nine hours and stay within the posted speed limits just has to be a man with no place in particular to go.

But there is country that interrupts this long barren stretch, interrupts at the beginning. From the time you cross the Colorado River and the Balcones Fault that slices Texas like a fifteen hundred mile blade, you have moved into the Hill Country. Farms and farming become occasional, and even a patch of land whose four corners can be seen all at once is nonetheless spoken of as a ranch, for this country is meant for sheep and goats, and cows and horses, and for deer and rattlesnakes and wild turkeys and armadillos. This is an outdoor land, where man confronts rather than lives with Nature.

It can be a deceptive land. Enter it after a rainy April, and the springs are flowing, the streams are rushing, the live oaks spread green canopies, and the field flowers wave in widespread beauty.

But come again, when it is September and days of clear blue skies and bright starry nights have succeeded each other weeks without end, with only now and then a solitary stray of a cloud to give hope without substance. Then you see how really shallow are the streams, how temporary are the springs, how thin the topsoil, and how shadeless the spidery mesquite and dull cedar. Life just seems to laze, things endure, and wait. Only the darting lizards, and the thousands of automobilists, the windows of their cars buttoned tight to hoard the artificial climate called air-conditioning, seem capable of much movement. Work goes on, and jobs get done, but mainly the thoughts are pointed north, waiting for that first breeze of fall to come gentling in.

Autumn brings some flame, particularly with the Spanish oak and the sumac. The colors, though, are burnished and muted rather than all fire and brilliance as in the country to the east of Austin or in such traditional broadleaf country as New Mexico's Red River Valley or New England's maple and elm paradises. And around the corner lies winter, which thrusts and surges, dropping temperatures overnight as much as sixty or seventy degrees. Then the Hill Country can look bleak, with all the stern strength of bleakness, but bleak just the same. And men get marooned by sleet and call to Blanco and to Harper that they won't be home tonight. That is, they call unless perhaps the lines are down from the weight of ice. Then the Department of Public Safety issues bulletins to stay off Highway 290 and all its feeding myriad of ranch roads and farm roads. And other men put on their foul weather gear, zipped to the neck and tight over the ears, then go out to protect livestock. The gentility of spring and the oven evenness of summer seem far away.

The Hill Country has more to it, however, than just the chances of geography and the caprices of weather. The Hill Country is also people. It is people who have had to grub for what they got, who have wrested from Nature rather than received from Nature. It is people who have learned to work and wait and believe that after the testing the good Lord would make something, rain most likely, turn up. Like hard workers, these people play hard when they have the opportunity. They know how to rejoice together, to share the good moments and to gloat in their triumph over protracted despair. They can suffer through, and they do.

Primarily they come from Anglo-Saxon, German, and Mexican stock. The most frequent names are names like Johnson, Weinheimer, or Flores. They do an adroit and effective job both of mingling and of maintaining their separate identities.

A Saturday night German dance behind Fischer's General Store is a latter twentieth-century version of an old-time frontier cabin-raising, except that beer replaces the rum. Joy reigns, and the whole family is invited to participate. The old folks do the schottische, the younger ones swing a bit, and three and four year olds are on the floor putting their little foot. It is community fun at its liveliest, and no one cares whether you speak with a straight Texas twang, pronounce your "f's" as if they were "pf's," or call out to Julio as if it were spelled "Hulio." The idea is that you are all God's creatures, from babes who can barely amble to octogenarians who can't walk much firmer.

Or if you don't want to dance, just drop in on Benno Engel's filling station (and it is not a service station), post office, and general store at Luckenbach. Benno is several generations removed from youth, and his father kept the store before him, so that it dates back well before the advent of the twentieth century. In the back room the men sit around on the hide-bottom chairs, themselves of a vintage redolent of memories, and talk over their beer on a Saturday night of how it was, how it is, and how it is going to be.

They may even bring up again the story of Jacob Brodbeck who taught over on South Grape Creek, where he married his pupil, Christine Sophie Behrens, who presented him with twelve children. As if that weren't enough, during the Civil War Brodbeck built a model airplane that flew, powered by clock springs. For twenty years he tried to take man off the ground, flying, you might say, in the face of all those who believed that God did not intend for man to have wings until he passed into the next world. The accounts of this flight vary, but undoubtedly Brodbeck did crash the silence of the Hill Country a third of a century before the Wright brothers took off from Kitty Hawk. He lived on until 1910, so that many of the people in their seventies and eighties remember him and still argue whether he was a genius or mad.

The Germans who settled the Hill Country came largely from the artisan class. They knew crafts. How well they would have made out in a land that was not naturally kind to farmers is arguable, but Brigham Young played an incidental role in helping these people achieve harmony with the land. Some Missouri Mormons, dissatisfied with the Prophet's leadership, turned southward and settled on the north edge of the Hill Country to duplicate the kind of community they had at Nauvoo and were to have later at Salt Lake City. When the German craftsmen, naive in thinking that this land had much use for their skills, showed an inability to cope with the land, their Mormon neighbors came down among them and taught them how this rocky land should be tilled. Undoubtedly the Mormons kept the Germans from starving in wholesale lots. The Mormon era is brief, for successive floods destroyed their mills and their community and sent them heading out of the Hill Country. But in their brief moment in Hill Country history, they too made a positive contribution.

Besides the hills purpling in the distance, the scrub oaks twisting without pattern, and the willows lining the creeks, one of the notable qualities of the Hill Country is its rocks. Stone lies just beneath the powdered topsoil, stone fences go on sometimes for miles until even from the vast comfort of a car you wonder how many thousands of man-hours went into placing those stones on stones, usually without mortar, and stone houses punctuate the landscape. Stonewall seems then not to have been named for a general in Virginia, but for the sometimes calcareous, sometimes flinty countryside. Particularly this is limestone country, with chalk cliffs, caves, and river banks that bespeak a geologic smallpox epidemic, so potted and pock-marked is the countryside. On the other hand, it was here that the people held firm when Texas participated almost gleefully in that great madness known as the Civil War. The people had come into this country believing that the United States offered a haven. Devoted in their belief, they could not sanction any movement to tear the

Union asunder. Despite intolerable pressure, they stood for their beliefs, and for their devotion to the principle of union they were harried, had their stock run off, saw their barns and houses burned, were even massacred, or forced to flee to Mexico until sanity returned to their neighbors. Yes, they too were stone walls, people whom no amount of abuse or confrontation could force off a road which they believed to be the right one.

The Hill Country then is sturdy country, carved out of wood and stone as well as that hallmark of pioneer Texas, hoof and horn. Whether the people built of log or stone, they built to last. In its genteel ruggedness the Hill Country has character. The limestone country may not have the granitic hardness of Vermont, the magnetic qualities of Upper Michigan's iron country, nor the high sheer cliffs of the towering Rockies. But the Hill Country manages to be both happy and durable, and its people reflect that mood.

JOE B. FRANTZ

THANKS

THE GERMANS IN TEXAS have received increasing attention in the past few years. A long-time basic book has been Rudolph L. Biesele's *The History of the German Settlements in Texas, 1831-1861*. Irene Marschall King's recent book on John Meusebach is quite helpful. For this particular work, *The History of Stonewall, Texas, 1860-1960*, compiled by The Stonewall Centennial History Committee, Hugo Weinheimer, Chairman; and John S. Moursund's *Blanco County Families for One Hundred Years* are especially valuable. A lion's share of the credit, or in one case, a lioness', belongs to Ruth Mathews, who works creatively and rapidly; James Alvis, who did a lot of the imaginative legwork and who thinks as he moves; to William Wittliff who is understanding; to the score or so of Hill Country people who took time to visit and to inform; and to those folks who have helped in many and varying ways: Maude Folmar, Henderson Shuffler, Ann Sanders, Bill Paschall, Liz Carpenter, Max Brooks, Frances Hudspeth. We thank them all sincerely.

JOE B. FRANTZ
J. ROY WHITE

THE HOUSES   PAISANO 2

MILLER CREEK HOUSE 4

STONE BUILDINGS 6

STONE CISTERN BUILDING 8

STONE BARN 10

STONE BUILDING WITH ARCHWAY 12

BOYHOOD HOME 14

THE LEWIS RANCH 16

ROUND MOUNTAIN STABLE 18

SANDY 20

SULTEMEIER HOUSE 22

HYE POST OFFICE 24

FRITZ LINDIG HOUSE 26

FRUIT STAND 28

THE HODGES HOUSE 30

THE HODGES BARN 32

SAUER HOMESTEAD 34

36 SAUER HOMESTEAD BARN & FENCES
38 ERWIN LINDIG HOUSE
40 ALBERT POST OFFICE
42 ALBERT SCHOOL
44 ALBERT ROAD LOG HOUSE
46 DANZ HOUSE
48 ALBERT NEBGEN HOME
50 STONE HOUSE
52 NUÑEZ HOUSE
54 SISTERDALE SCHOOL
56 RUDY'S BARNS
58 LUCKENBACH POST OFFICE
60 BLUMENTHAL
62 FARMHOUSE
64 FREDERICKSBURG FACHVERK HOUSE
66 FREDERICKSBURG SHOP
68 FREDERICKSBURG SUNDAY HOUSE, A.D. 1968

LIMESTONE and LOG

PAISANO
near Circleville

J. FRANK DOBIE knew more tales of Texas and the Southwest than any man who ever lived, even including Bigfoot Wallace. In his later years, when he could no longer visit regularly the old family ranch down in the Nueces country, he looked around for a place within easy driving distance of Austin. The result was Paisano, a small ranch known to lovers of literature and admirers of Dobie. At the big house a man could sit on the gallery and enjoy good talk. Or if it was cold, he'd go inside and sit before the rock fireplace, while Mr. Frank fed the fire with mesquite logs. The walls were covered with Dobie gear—bridle, hay hook, arrowhead collection, horns over the door, Dobie's bootjack. An old carved wooden chair, purchased by Mrs. Dobie when the Driskill Hotel in Austin decided to modernize, sits there with a big D carved on the back. The D is for Driskill, but it looks as if it should stand for Dobie. One of the bonuses which Dobie received from Paisano, at the opposite end of his place, was a log cabin of square logs, hand-hewn. Inside is a stone fireplace and chimney. The logs, of cedar, dovetail. In the rainy season one has to talk a bit louder, because Barton Creek falls and rushes just below the main house, and adds the kind of noise that Dobie, who could not tolerate the noises of man or machinery, liked to listen to. Paisano is now a writer's retreat, which is what Dobie wanted before he died and which is exactly what it seems meant for, for it was a retreat for one fine writer while Dobie owned it.

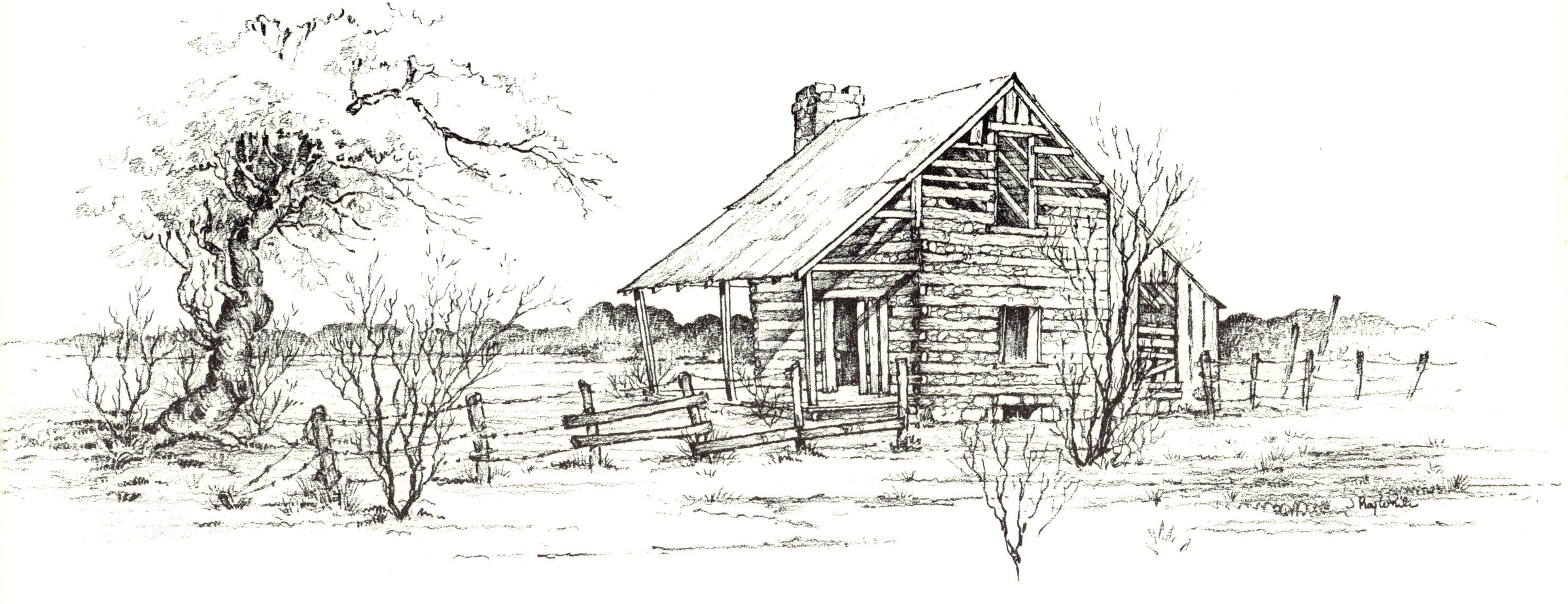

MILLER CREEK HOUSE

ORIGINALLY this was called Mill Seat and again, Cedar Falls. W. D. Felps and his wife, Lissie, operated the mill about the time of the Civil War. It ran twenty-four hours a day to grind corn and wheat. Mrs. Felps once proved a hindrance when her hoopskirt caught in the mill machinery. It not only stopped the belts, but broke several of her bones and cut off her thumb. W. D. Felps' brother Tom and his wife Lisa were fishing at Miller's Creek when a Negro boy rode up to warn them of an Indian attack. Tom, who had red hair, was killed immediately, but Lisa, who had long black hair, was scalped and killed later. The Negro boy escaped. The house itself has large 4 x 4 hand-hewn wooden lintels above the windows and doors. A large semicircular toothed iron wheel serves as a lintel for the fireplace. Some people think it may be a piece of old milling machinery. Outside, a hand-cut millrace can be seen in the limestone next to the creek. Just below the falls there is a hole in the bottom of the creek caused by the water falling from the mill wheel through the years.

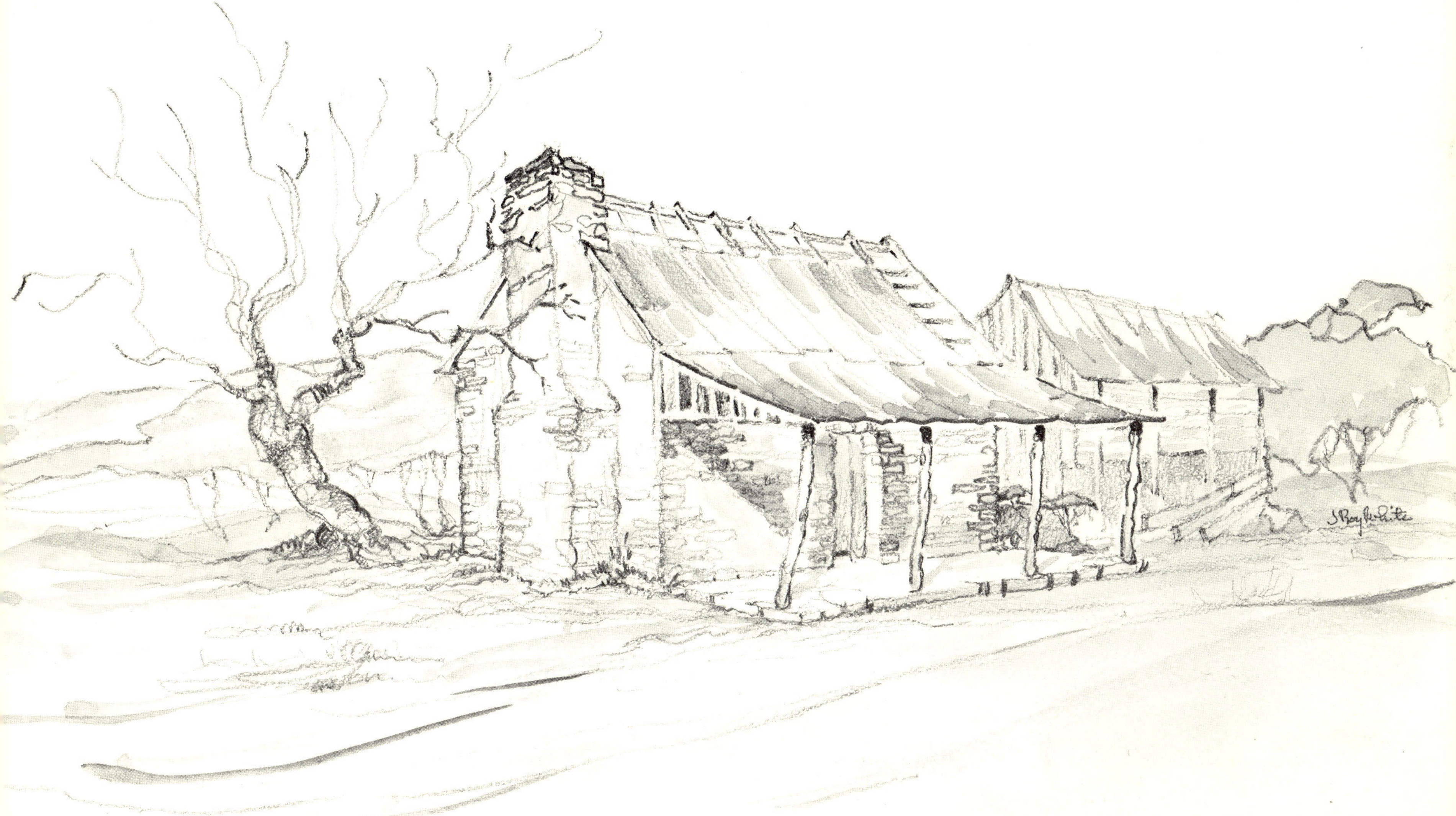
J Roy White

STONE BUILDINGS
Johnson City

HERE IT ALL BEGAN. James Polk Johnson, who had come from Alabama to serve Texas in the Army of the Confederacy and to trail cattle to Kansas following the Civil War, bought this land both to farm and to found a community. The community of Johnson City is larger than it was when James Polk Johnson had his dream, but not so much that the visitor cannot transport himself back to those days when young Johnson, newly married, listed his property as four horses, seven cattle, and three mules, an entire estate worth three hundred and ninety-five dollars.

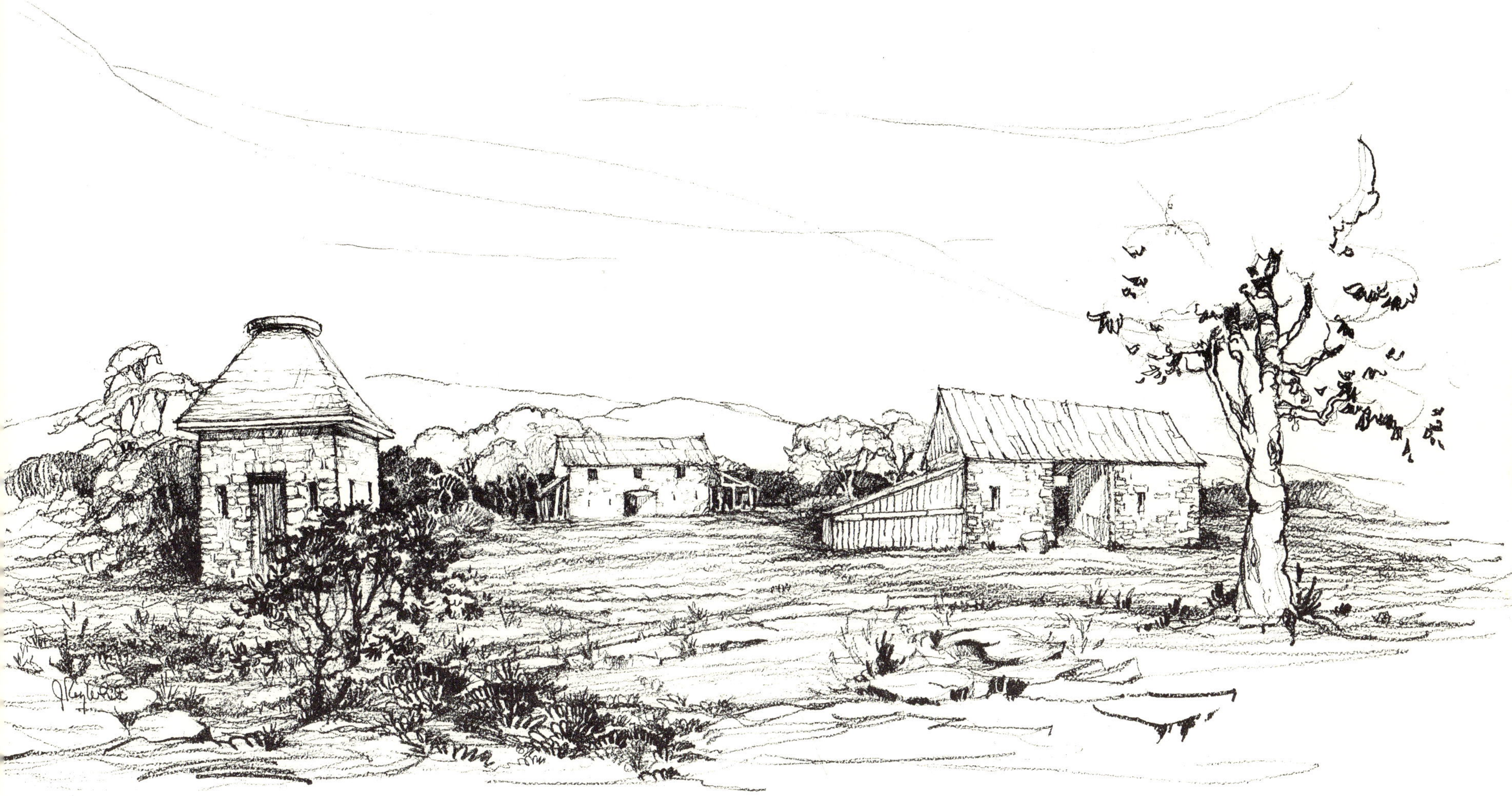

STONE CISTERN BUILDING
Johnson City

FRED BRUCKNER JR. now lives on the old John Bruckner Sr. property. Fred Bruckner Jr. thinks that the cistern house may once have been a smokehouse. Whichever it was, either would have been necessary. In a land of now-and-then rainfall, cisterns are essential. The authors have poked their noses into the cistern house and did not detect that pungent, nostalgic smokehouse odor. Since both grew up with smokehouses, we believe that smokehouse smells are eternal and satisfying, and so we are satisfied to call this simply a stone cistern house.

In the background can be seen a house, lived in today by Fred Bruckner Jr., and built over the original Johnson log house, erected about 1872-1873. Probably these two properties occupy the first site of habitation which we now know as Johnson City.

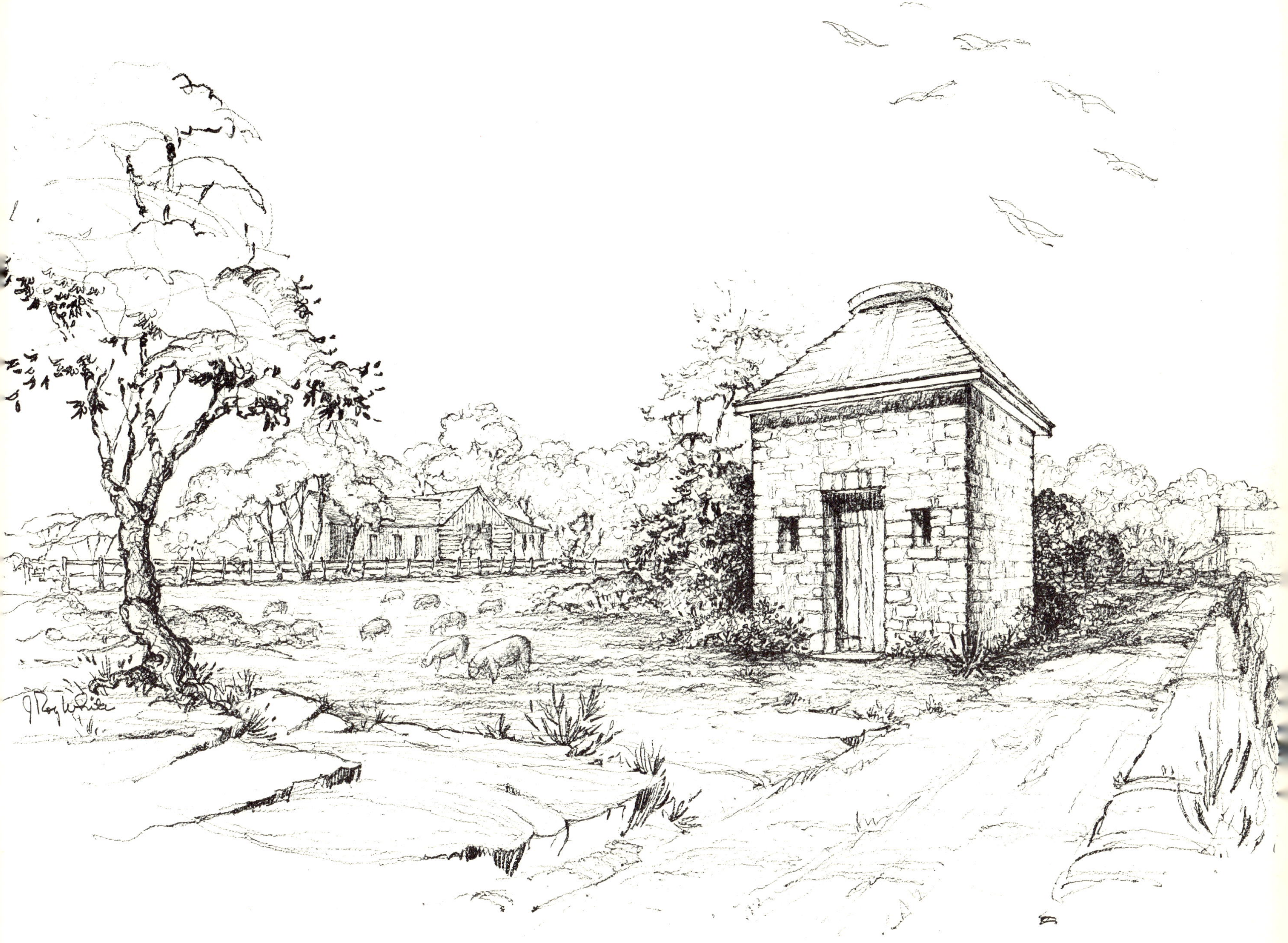
J Roy White

STONE BARN
Johnson City

JUST A LITTLE GENEALOGY to illustrate how people come together to build for now and later: John Bruckner Sr. was born in 1842 in Gefell, Voightland, Schliezer Street, in the Saxony portion of East Germany which now lies beyond the Iron Curtain. Before he was eighteen, he had landed at Galveston, and eventually he married Emma Schuhmann, whose family had come from Oberschiebe by Schiebenberg, also in Saxony. In 1882 John Bruckner Sr. bought three hundred and twenty acres of land from James Polk Johnson, although he did not move on to the land for another eleven years. But his brother and sister, Christian and Karolina, lived on the Johnson property; to improve the place, John Sr. had a large stone barn constructed. Some people call the barn the Old Stone Fort, but it was built long after the Indians ceased to roam in that part of the Hill Country. It was built as a barn, and it was built to last. It has lasted.

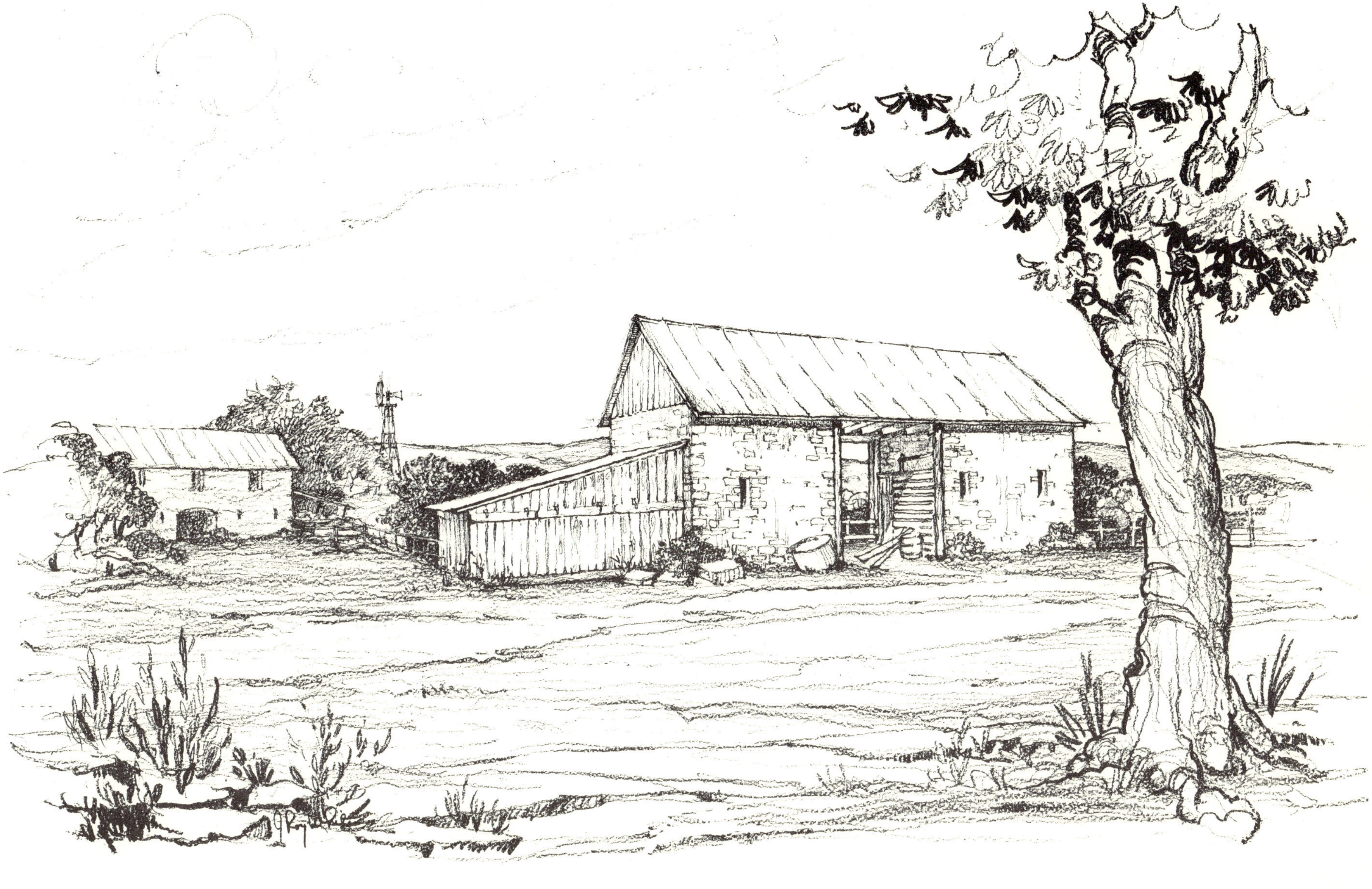

STONE BUILDING
WITH ARCHWAY
Johnson City

SAMUEL EALY JOHNSON SR. was an uncle of James Polk. He had come into Blanco County as a single young man looking for some way to get ahead with horses and cattle. He had a son with the same name who in turn named his eldest son Lyndon Baines. All three generations knew stone barns with steep roofs, usually of tin, and lean-to sheds either open or boarded up at either end. They were useful in 1859; they will be just as useful if men are still farming and tending cattle in the year 2000.

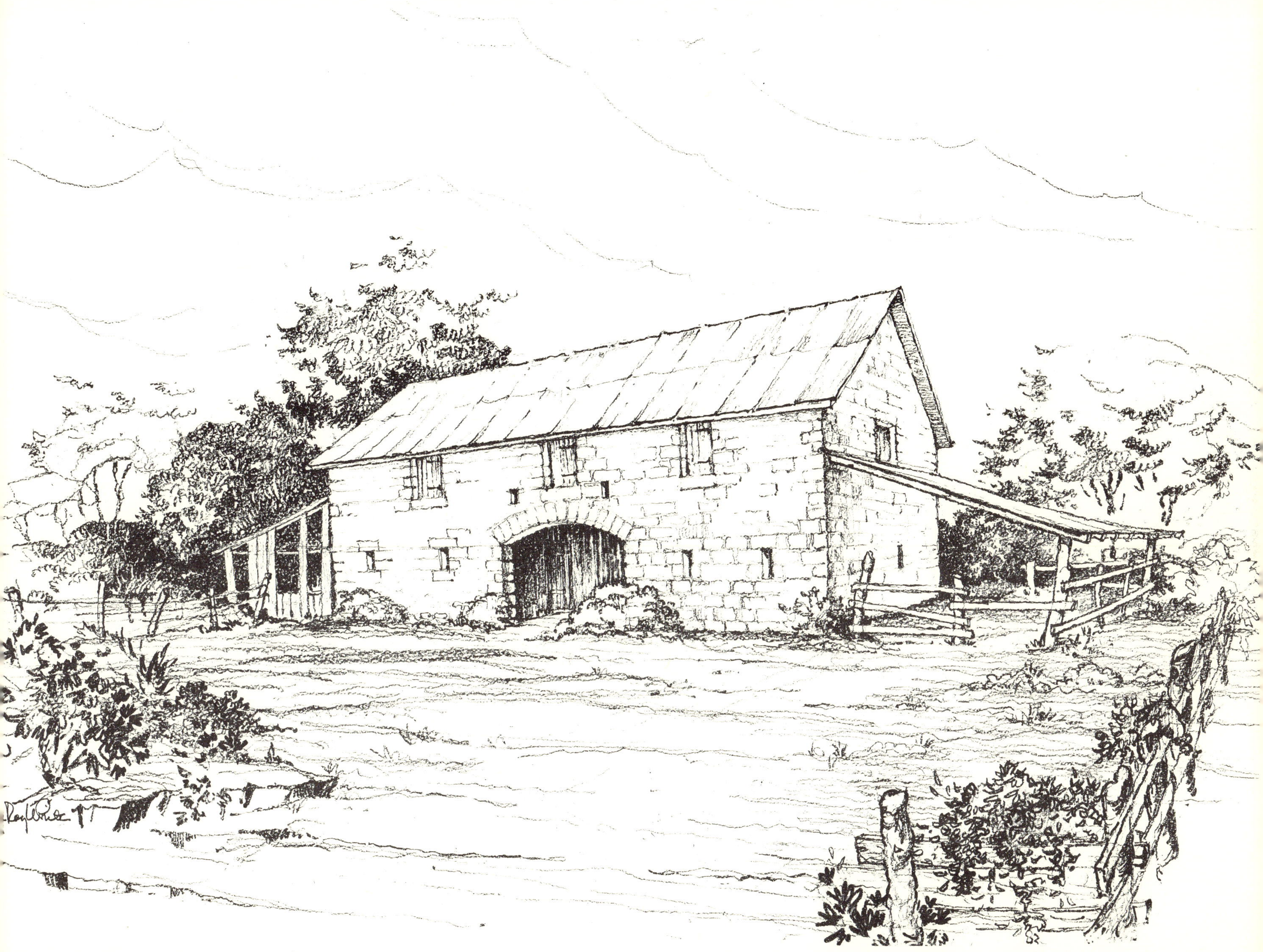

BOYHOOD HOME
Johnson City

AS THE YEARS WENT BY, Johnson City took on the appearance of civilization. In 1886 a substantial residence was built and, in the manner which has been fashionable since the days of early New England, the house was added-to a score of years later. Then in 1913 Sam Ealy Johnson, Jr. brought his small brood of a wife and three children to live there. Two more children were to be born in the nearly quarter of a century that the house was occupied by the Johnsons. It was here too that a young boy played from the time he was five years old until he left home to be his own man. The old well, the zinnias, crape myrtles, stands of ferns, and hanging baskets of "wandering Jew" are redolent of those innocent days that marked the first quarter of the twentieth century. A boy could run, roll and wrestle in the grass, climb and fall from trees, or swing in an abandoned rubber tire or a double swing. It was a spacious world in which to grow up.

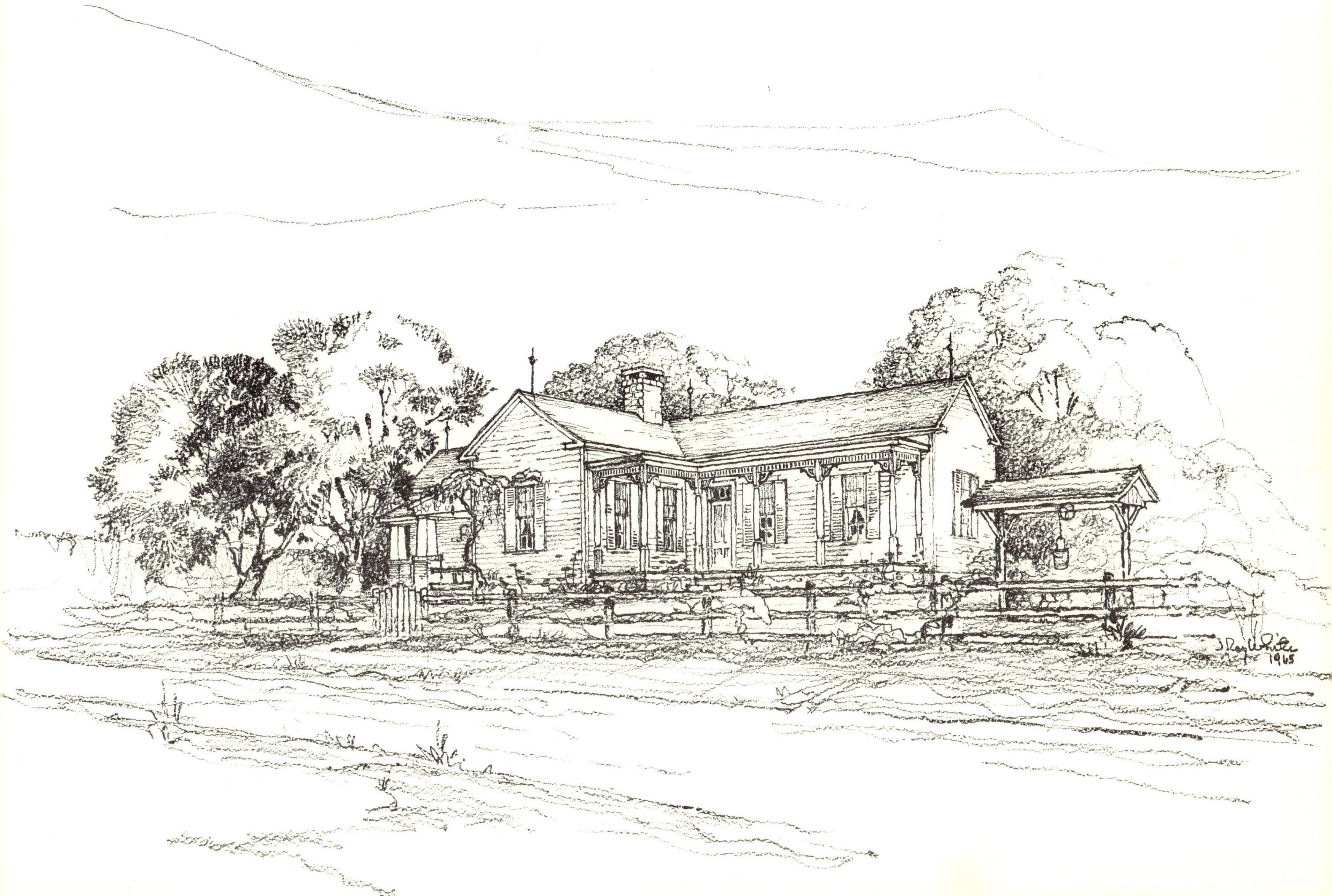
J. Ray White
1965

THE LEWIS RANCH
near Johnson City

IN THE SOUTH CORNER WALL of the front porch of the Lewis Ranch House is a bullet hole. It all started when Bige Hopper, who trapped, traded, and fiddled, took offense at Al Tobin, who owned the house. Hopper thought that Tobin was eyeing his wife, and so in the fashion of the time he followed Tobin home, shot him in the arm, and chased him around the house. It was probably all good clean fun. Tobin, however, was plagued by a dark star. He adopted a boy who helped as a field hand. One day while Tobin had his head down drinking water, the boy removed his benefactor from this world with still another bullet.

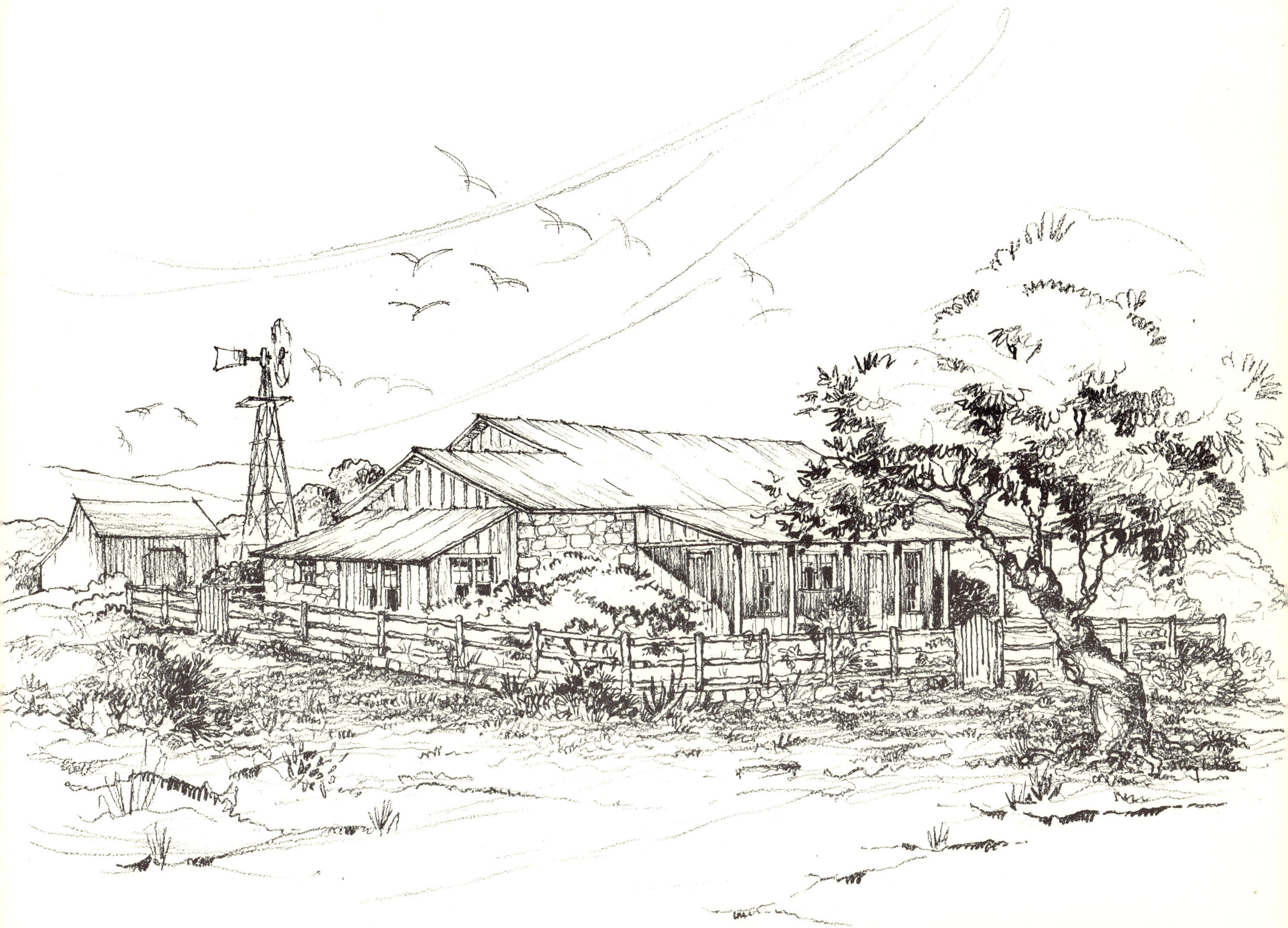

ROUND MOUNTAIN STABLE

THIS STABLE and the lodge, which can barely be discerned beyond it, are remarkable buildings, perhaps because they were built by a woman, Mrs. Elitha Martin, nearly a hundred years ago. Above the windows and doors are large lintel stones. The stable doorway is marked by a huge segmental arch. The roof overhang on the stable has carved wooden supports. Back of the lodge is a stone-lined cistern and well. A rusty pump stands near the road at the front of the stable, the last reminder that here stood a blacksmith's shop. The room above the livery stable was used for meetings by the usual solid people, the Woodmen of the World, the Masons, and the voters at election time. The other building was a stage stop on the way to Austin. The markings of the old stage road can still be seen, especially where the stage had to plunge through the creek that runs alongside the inn.

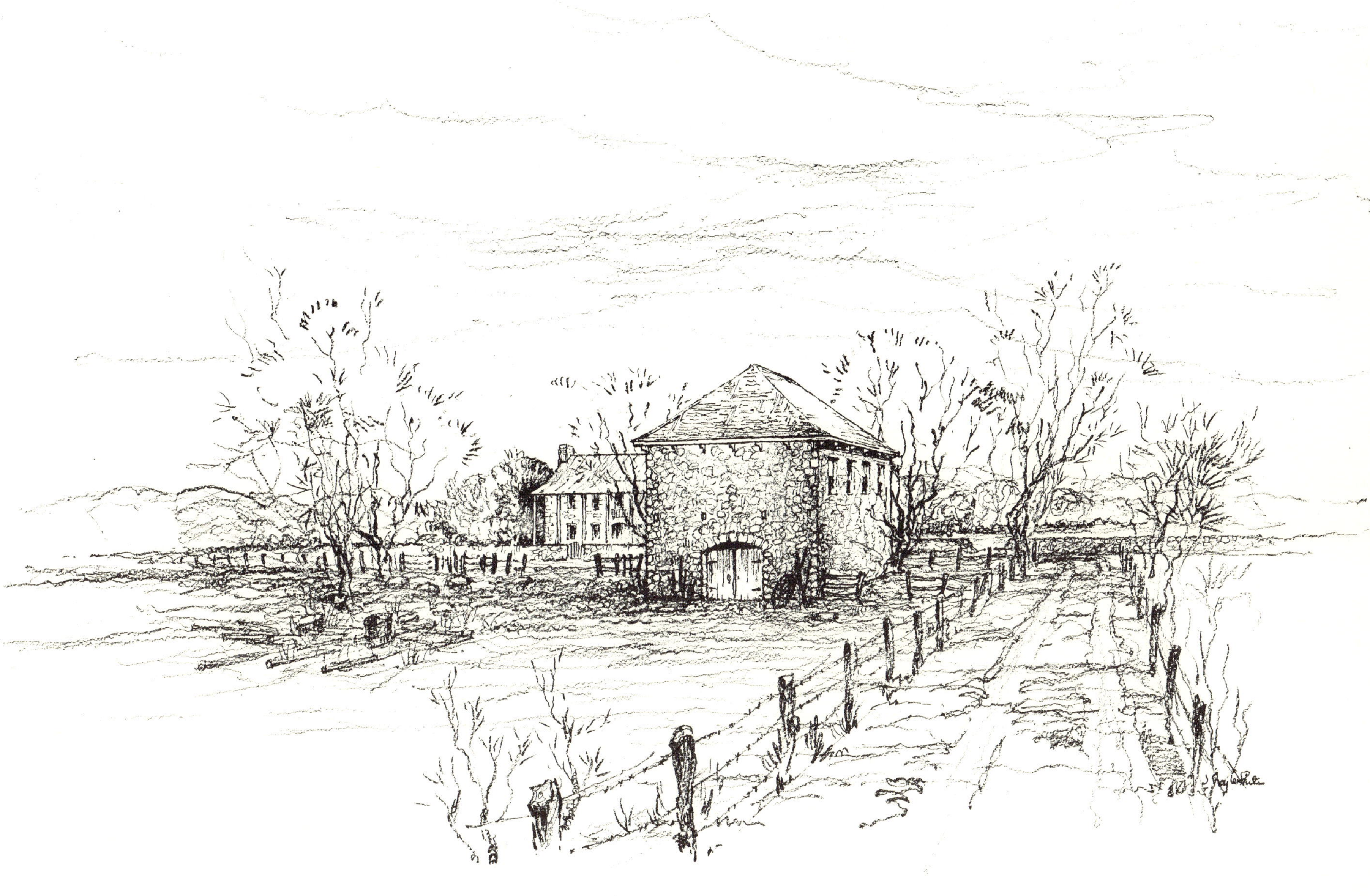

SANDY

SANDY had its first post office in a log cabin which in time also became a general store. At one time its inventory included two hundred barrels of flour, along with the usual nails, horseshoes, and axes which meant so much to this countryside. Sandy knew its cattle drives but even better it knew its turkey drives. Sometimes flocks of turkeys were driven as much as twenty-five miles to market. The first resident of Sandy's cemetery, a man named Hines, was killed by Indians on Hickory Creek. About 1890 a Sandy resident was lynched, but a story that Sandy residents would rather tell is about how in 1914 Sam Pearson and his family moved off to Oklahoma. On the ferry across the Red River, they missed their dog who had been with them when they boarded the ferry. Two months later the dog showed up at the Sandy Post Office.

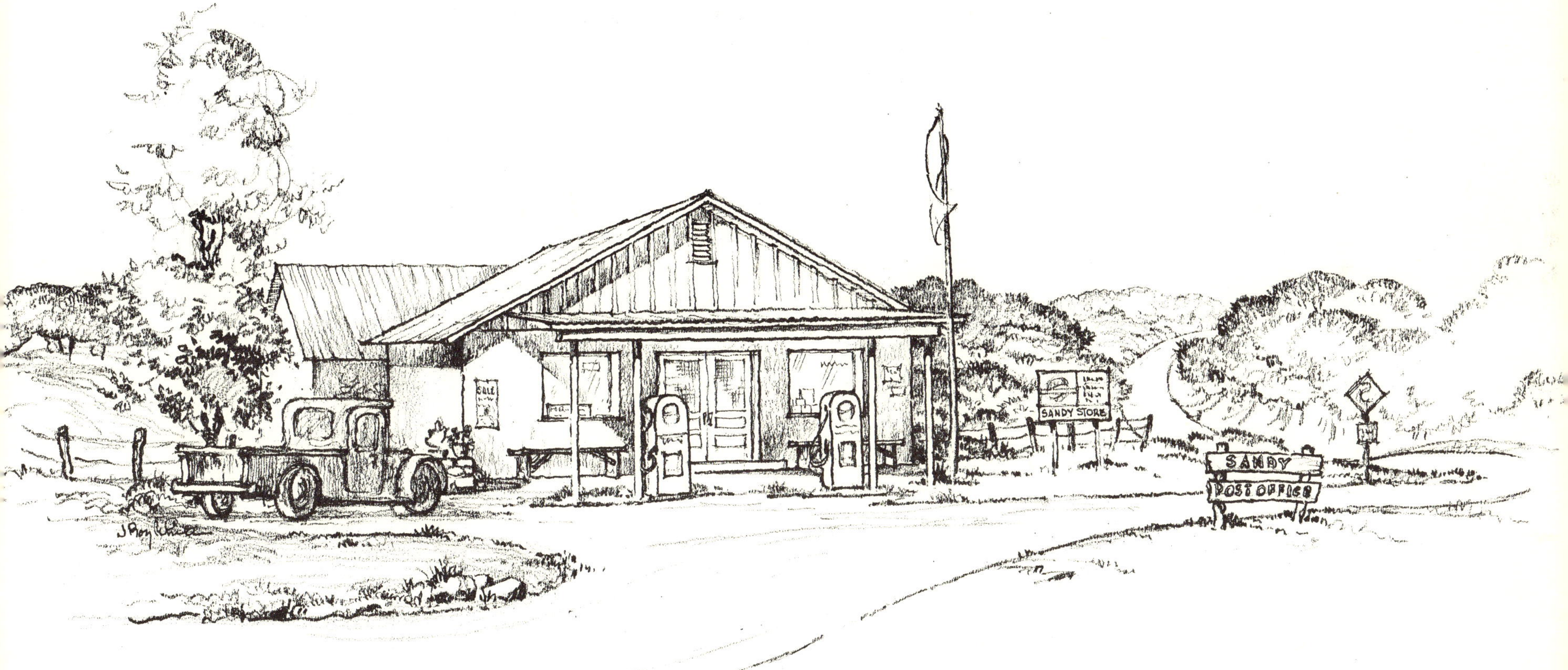
SALE
SANDY STORE
SANDY
POST OFFICE

SULTEMEIER HOUSE
near Sandy

JOSEPH P. CRIDER entered Texas from Missouri during its days as an independent republic. About 1881 he built this house. While his family resided here, they carried fresh eggs about four miles on horseback to Sandy, a business with all the promise of great wealth as a lemonade stand at the Gillespie County Fair, for the eggs brought five cents a dozen. The Criders reputedly had the largest sheep barn for miles around, so spacious that a wagon and team could be turned around inside it.

About fifty yards from the Crider home, a small stone house was built over a cold clear spring that bubbles right out of the rock. Like other spring houses it was a natural summer refrigerator for milk, butter, and cheese.

Here as elsewhere a landscape feature, so common as to go unnoticed by dry-land Texans, are the hordes and hillocks of cactus. Probably nowhere do the prickly pear grow more luxuriantly and more irregularly than in the Hill Country. In the spring they make small hillocks of yellow across the countryside, and as the summer comes on, their *tunas* or pears, turn a bright red, then a dull brown, and finally a somber purple. One roadside merchant, who developed a national business selling prickly pear to chain stores, has observed that his two greatest friends are women and water. Between them, he avers, they rot out his product and keep the demand ever constant. Prickly pear flourishes best when it is not wanted.

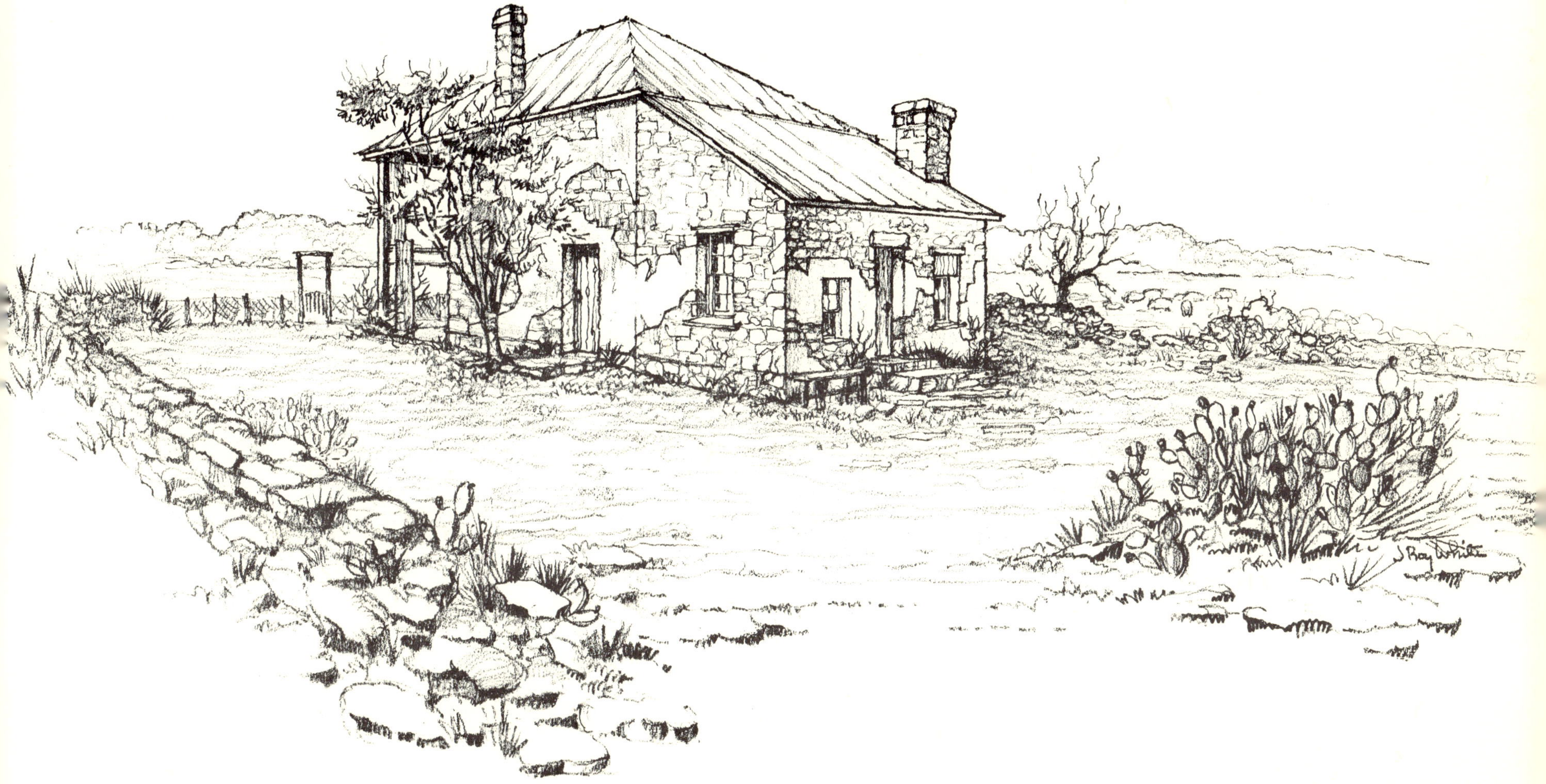
J Roy White

HYE POST OFFICE

THE HYE POST OFFICE looks as if it were newly painted and festooned for a Bavarian festival. Apparently it looked like that as far back as 1904, when it was first built. With unmatched gingerbread, it insists once again that the best post offices are located in general stores, this one run by Levi A. Deike, who has been postmaster and storekeeper for more than a third of a century. You can no longer buy calico and horse collars, but the original spool and thread chest and a big revolving bolt chest bring back the days which have passed. Hye Brown came here in 1880. He went broke twice, once because of high water, but he stuck it out for forty years.

Two national figures have had an association with Hye. On November 3, 1965, on the Hye Post Office front porch, Lawrence F. O'Brien was sworn in as Postmaster General of the United States. Some decades earlier a little tad, all of four years old, mailed his first letter at this post office. He grew into the man who appointed Postmaster General O'Brien.

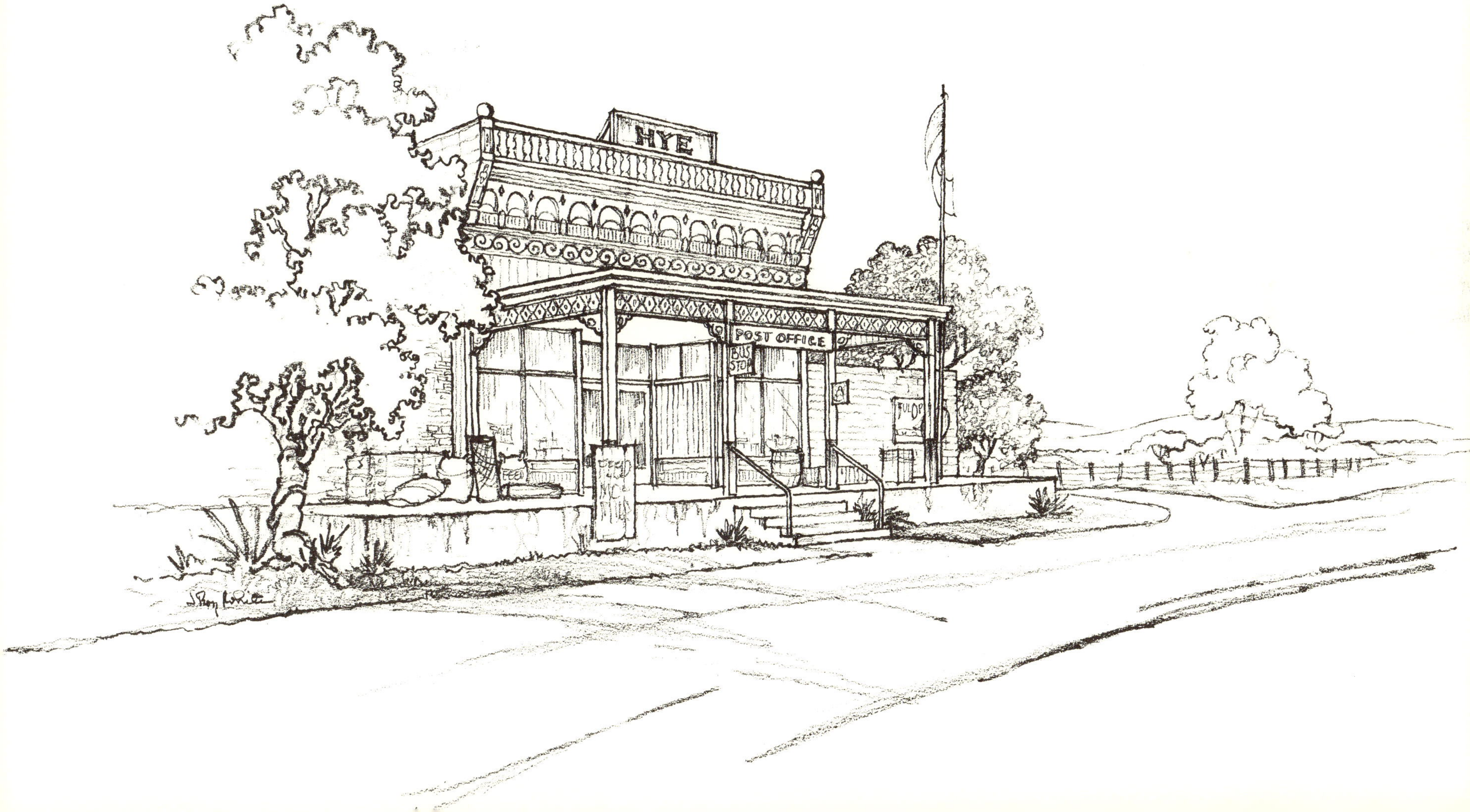
HYE
POST OFFICE
BUS STOP

FRITZ LINDIG HOUSE
near Hye

FRITZ LINDIG built his house in the late 1880's on a four hundred and three-acre plot. Over the years he produced cotton, corn, hay, and cattle, and he made them pay. The story-and-a-half house has an upstairs bedroom. The limestone walls run thick here—sixteen inches thick—and neither the winter winds nor the summer stillness can penetrate. But if the walls sweat or otherwise grow damp, then life in a house like this has its clammy spells.

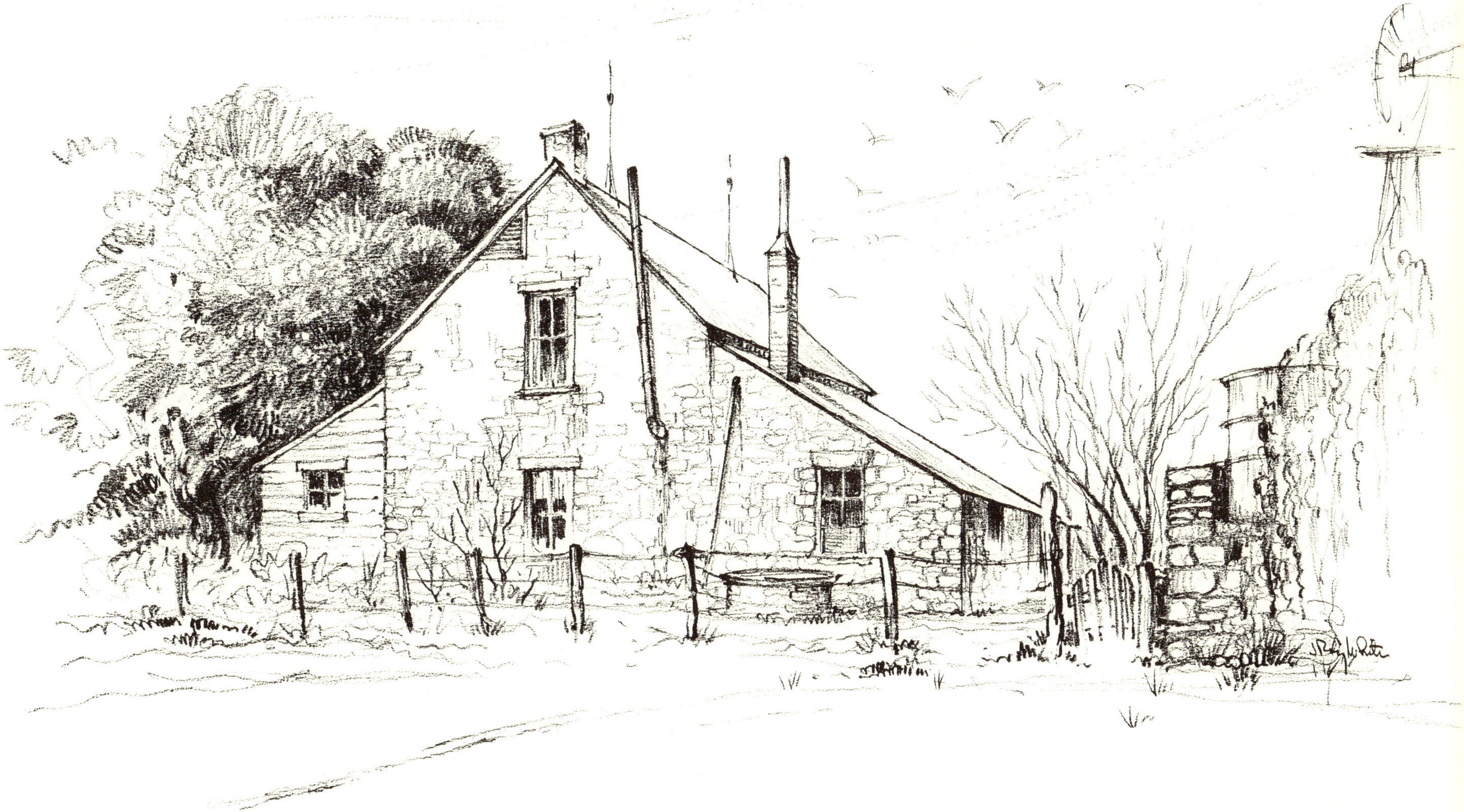

FRUIT STAND
Rocky Creek

THIS IS PEACHTREE COUNTRY, about the only type of orchard that flourishes in the Hill Country. In the spring the countryside has great patches of pink blossoms intermingling with the new green of the hills and trees, and the blues, reds, yellows, and purples of the field flowers. Hill Country peaches, show specimens or not, are exceedingly juicy and succulent. They make an excellent brandy which is greatly prized throughout Central Texas. An evidence of its quality is seen in the fact that during the brandy season some Germans will even forego their beer for a little brandy. There is no higher tribute. This is also fine pecan country, and roadside stands offer several varieties of this meaty nut. Melons and cantaloupes can also be bought at roadside stands, along with various other truck. It all adds to the kaleidoscope of color that one can see in the Hill Country in the summer and early autumn.

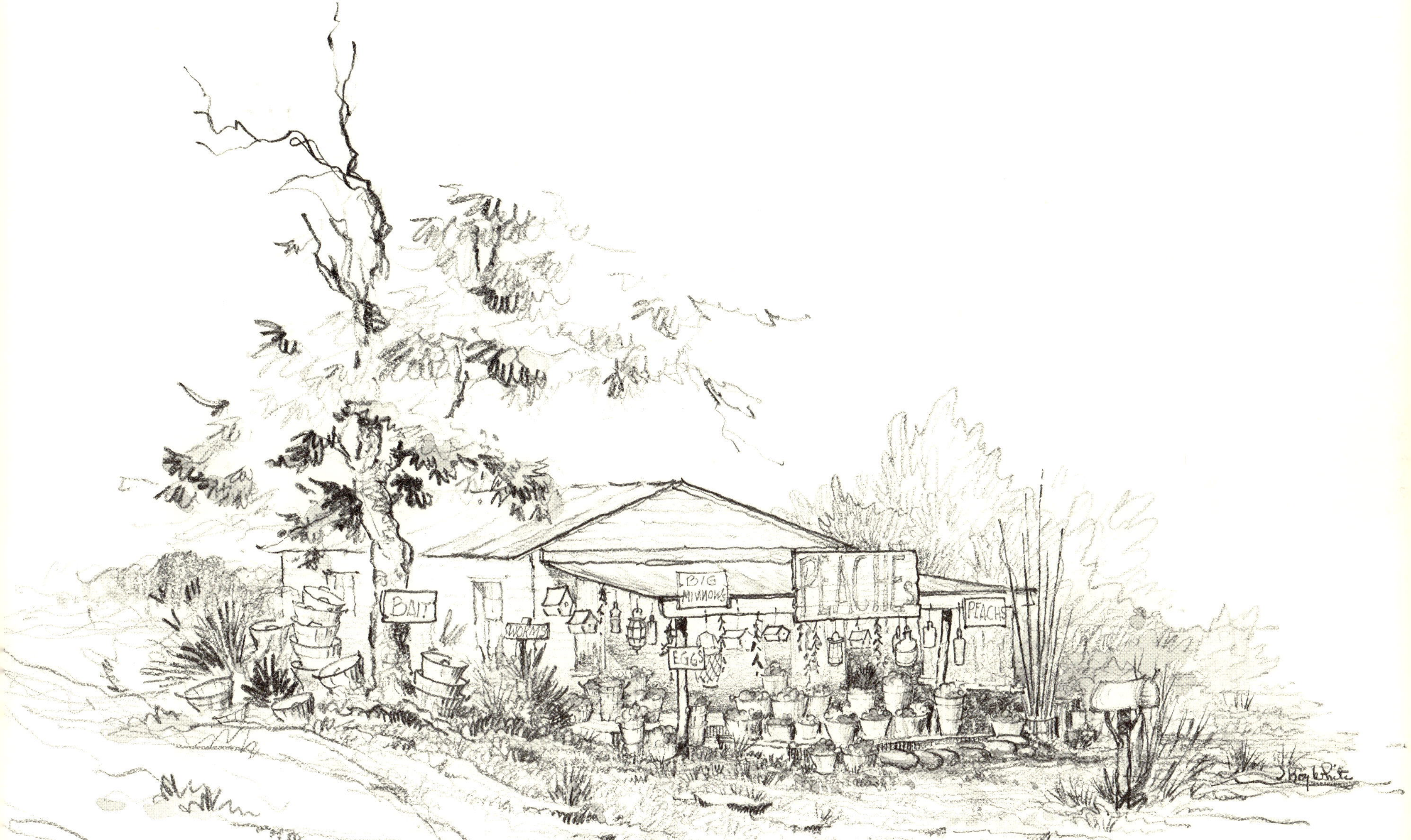
BAIT
WORMS
BIG MINNOWS
PEACHES
PEACHS
EGGS

THE HODGES HOUSE
on Ranch Road 1

ORIGINALLY the Hodges house had two rooms downstairs and two upstairs, with a porch for each floor and outside stairs to the second floor. As the owners grew in substance, the house was enlarged. It still has a cistern in the basement. Although Christian Lindig quarried the stone which faces the Hodges house, Mr. and Mrs. Hodges hauled the stone themselves. Mrs. Hodges' vivid memory goes back to 1952 when the river flooded until the house was an island in water at least a foot deep. When the waters receded, catfish were caught in the basement.

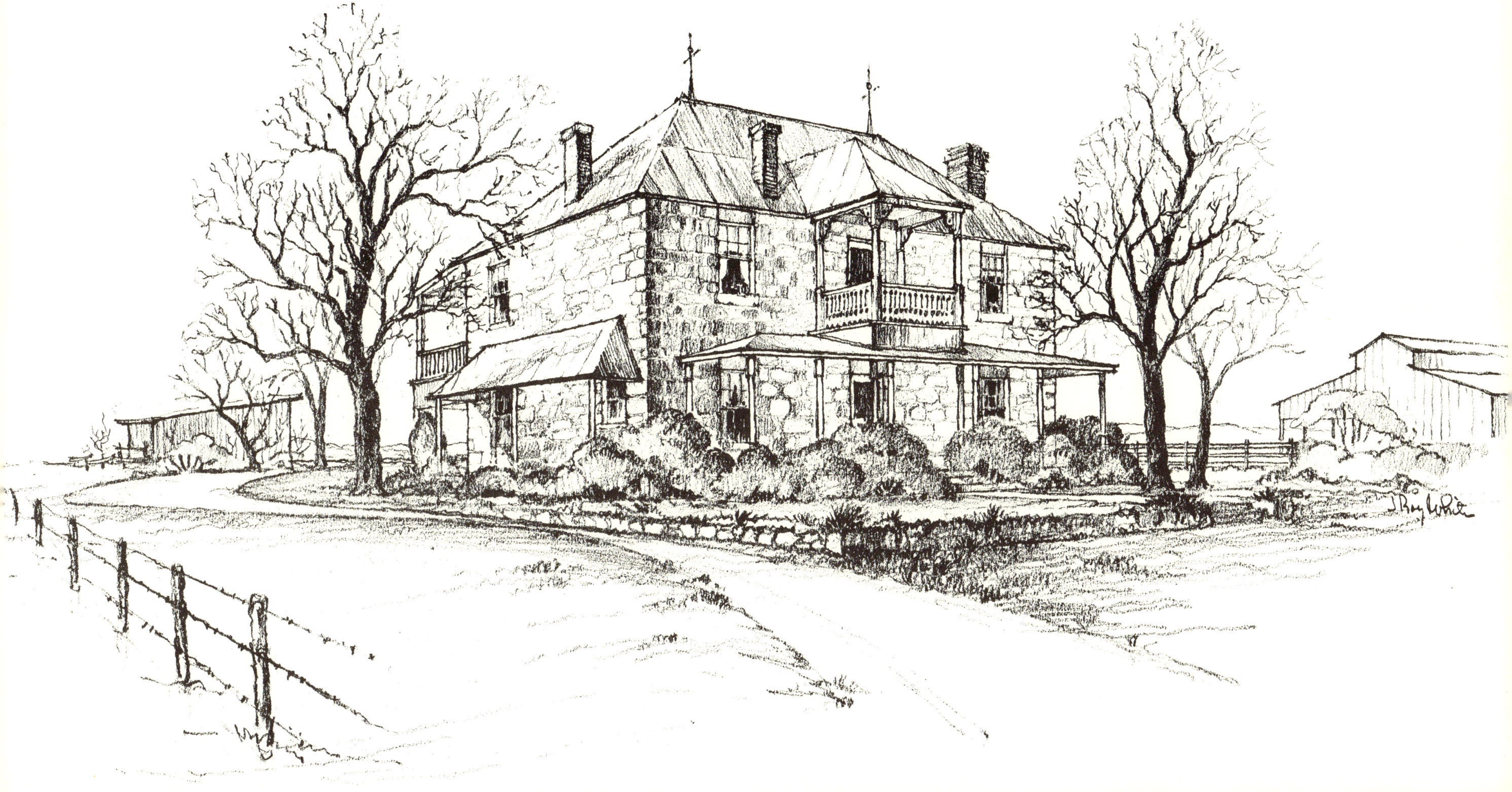

THE HODGES BARN
on Ranch Road 1

IN A.D. 1968 Mrs. Emery Hodges was ninety-three years old. A widow for twenty years, she still lives on the old home place, and remembers how it was in other generations. The barn itself has that clutter and richness which accompanies a going concern. Good barns in America belong to the country from Illinois to Maine, and are seldom seen on the places of working farmers outside those areas. The Hodges barn is a good barn on a Texas farm belonging to a working lady.

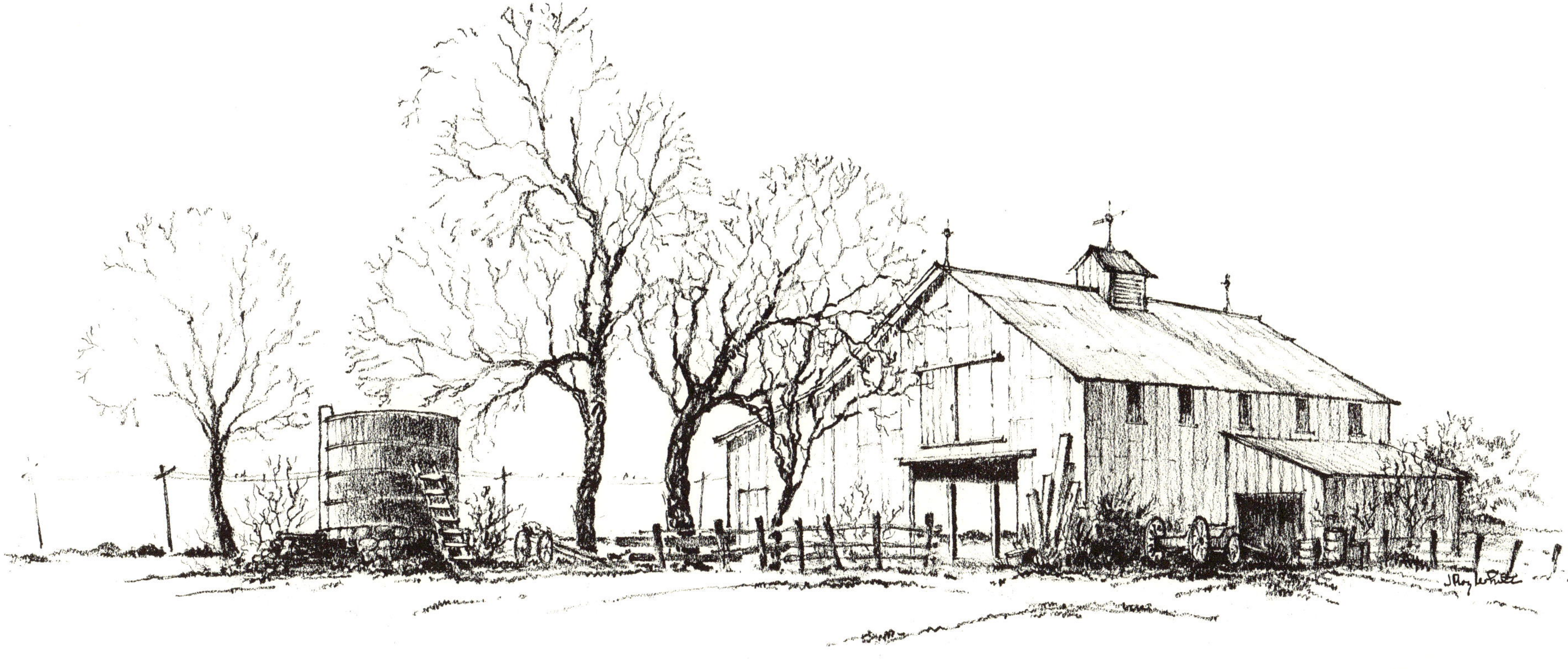

SAUER HOMESTEAD
near Stonewall

THE SAUER HOMESTEAD is really a small compound of buildings. Probably the Sauers first lived in the small stone building along the west fence line before moving into the larger house now known as the old home place. Here Frederick Sauer farmed and raised cattle and sheep while his wife gave him a family of ten children, including several sons to plow, carry stones, milk cows, and cut wood. Perhaps some were even old enough to help build this house, with its loft and its stone smokehouse to the rear. There was game in the sparse woods, and fish in the Pedernales, and growing children all over the rocky terrain. You could never have convinced the Sauers of the isolation of the Hill Country rural scene.

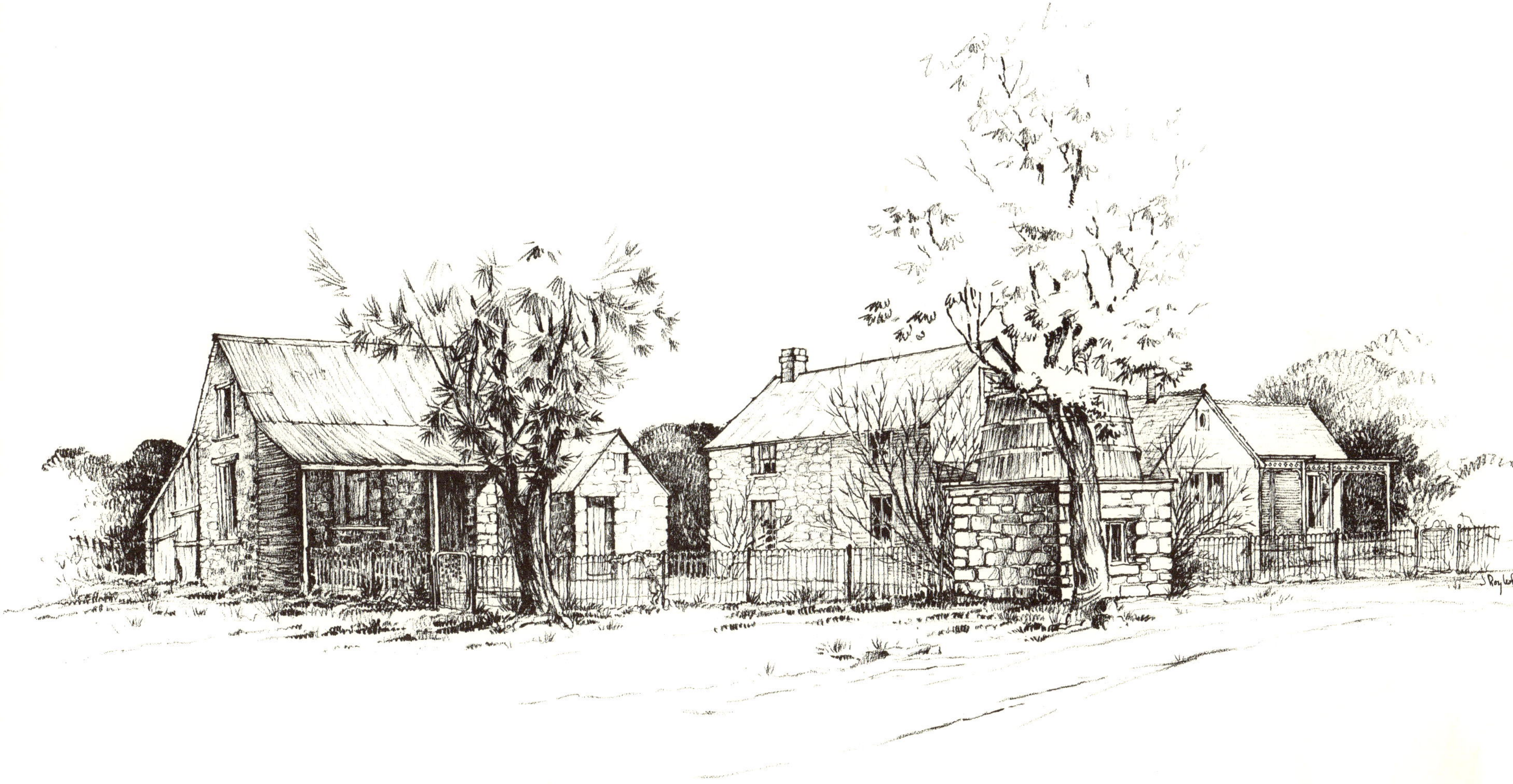

SAUER HOMESTEAD
BARN & FENCES
near Stonewall

FOR A COMMUNITY as tiny as Stonewall, the town has produced more than its share of people of significance. One of these is Emil Sauer, who lived in Stonewall through his thirteenth year, when he enrolled in Fredericksburg High School. He then taught for about three years in the area. After graduating from the University of Texas, he found his way back to Fredericksburg as superintendent of schools. But like another famous son, Emil Sauer thought his service lay outside the Hill Country. Consequently he entered the diplomatic service, and became the United States consul to such places as Bagdad, Goteborg, Sweden, Cologne, Maricaibo (where he met his future wife, Victoria Vale of Colombia), Copenhagen, Coblenz, Frankfurt, and Rio. He was in Frankfurt when the Second World War broke out and lived through forty-four nights of British air raids there. This was the boy who used to hang on these fences and bring the hay to the horses in this barn.

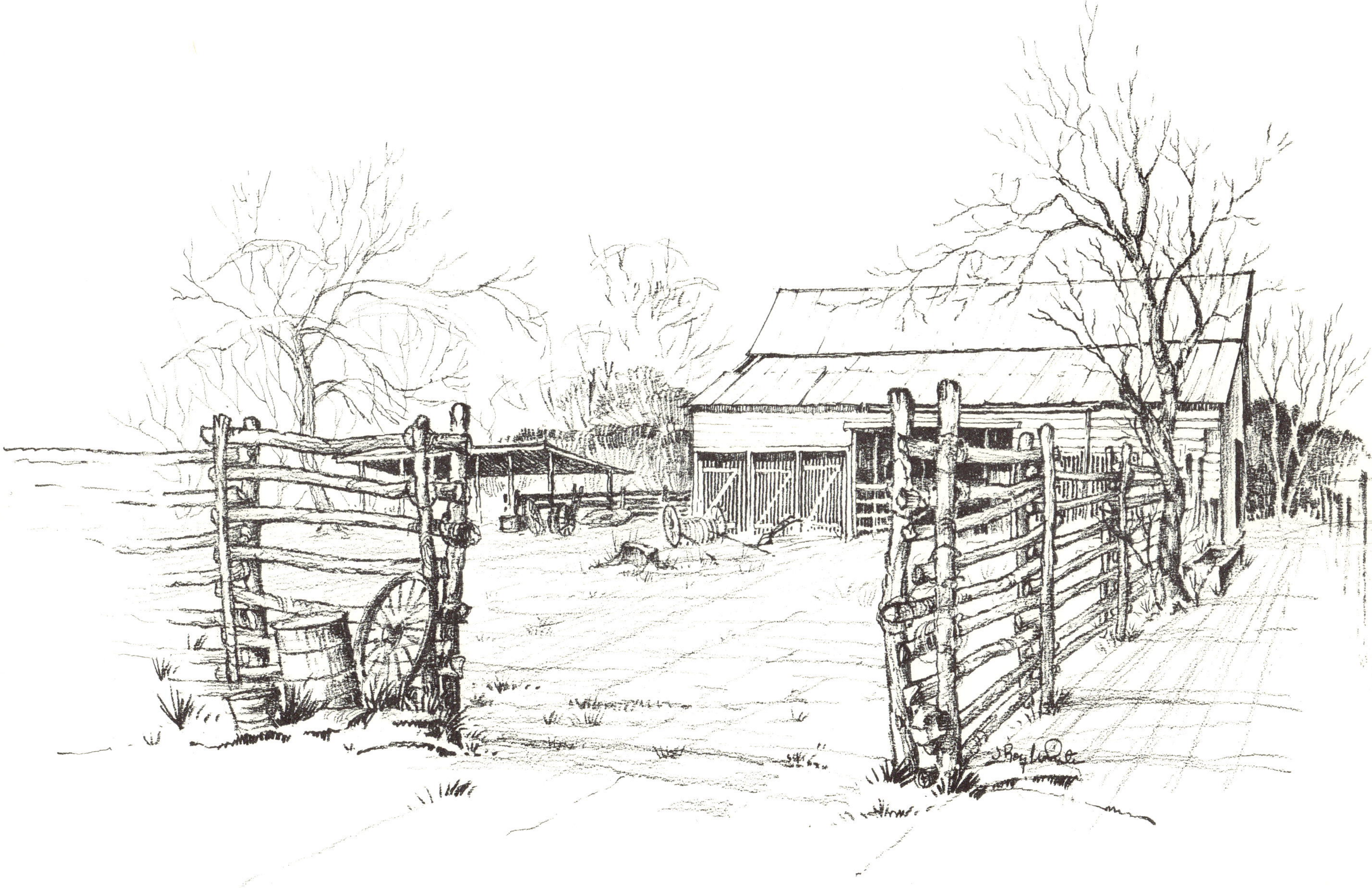

ERWIN LINDIG HOUSE
Albert Road

WHEN ANDRES LINDIG built this house in 1876, the land was completely open. The family could travel to Albert without encountering a single fence. Hay was cut by hand with a sickle, in a fashion that had not changed since the days of the Bible, that fundamental book which graced the homes of these pious, toiling, happy husbandmen. Like their stone houses, these people were built on solid bedrock, perhaps even more firm than the limestone bedrock which held their homes.

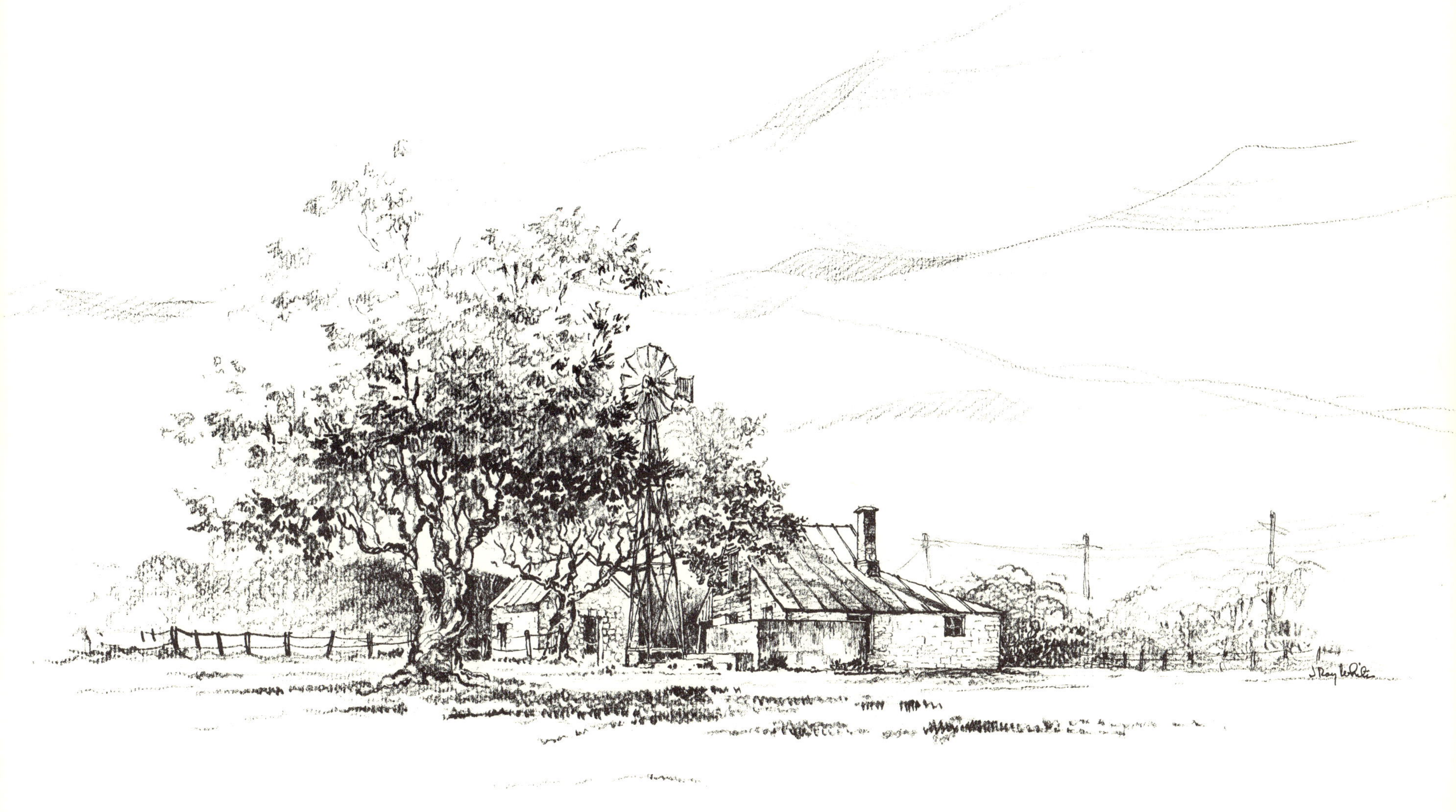
J Ray White

ALBERT POST OFFICE

ALBERT LUCKENBACH was a rancher and stockman. When the Engel family decided it was time to petition for a post office, one of the Engel girls was engaged to Albert. When she was chosen postmistress, she named the post office Luckenbach, to the great disappointment of the Engel family, which then and now is the cornerstone of that community. The postmistress married Albert Luckenbach and in time they moved to a new community which was seeking a post office. Again the young lady was chosen to be postmistress, and was given the honor of naming the new post office. She chose the name of Albert. Thus Albert Luckenbach is one of those few people in the world for whom two neighboring post offices and towns are named.

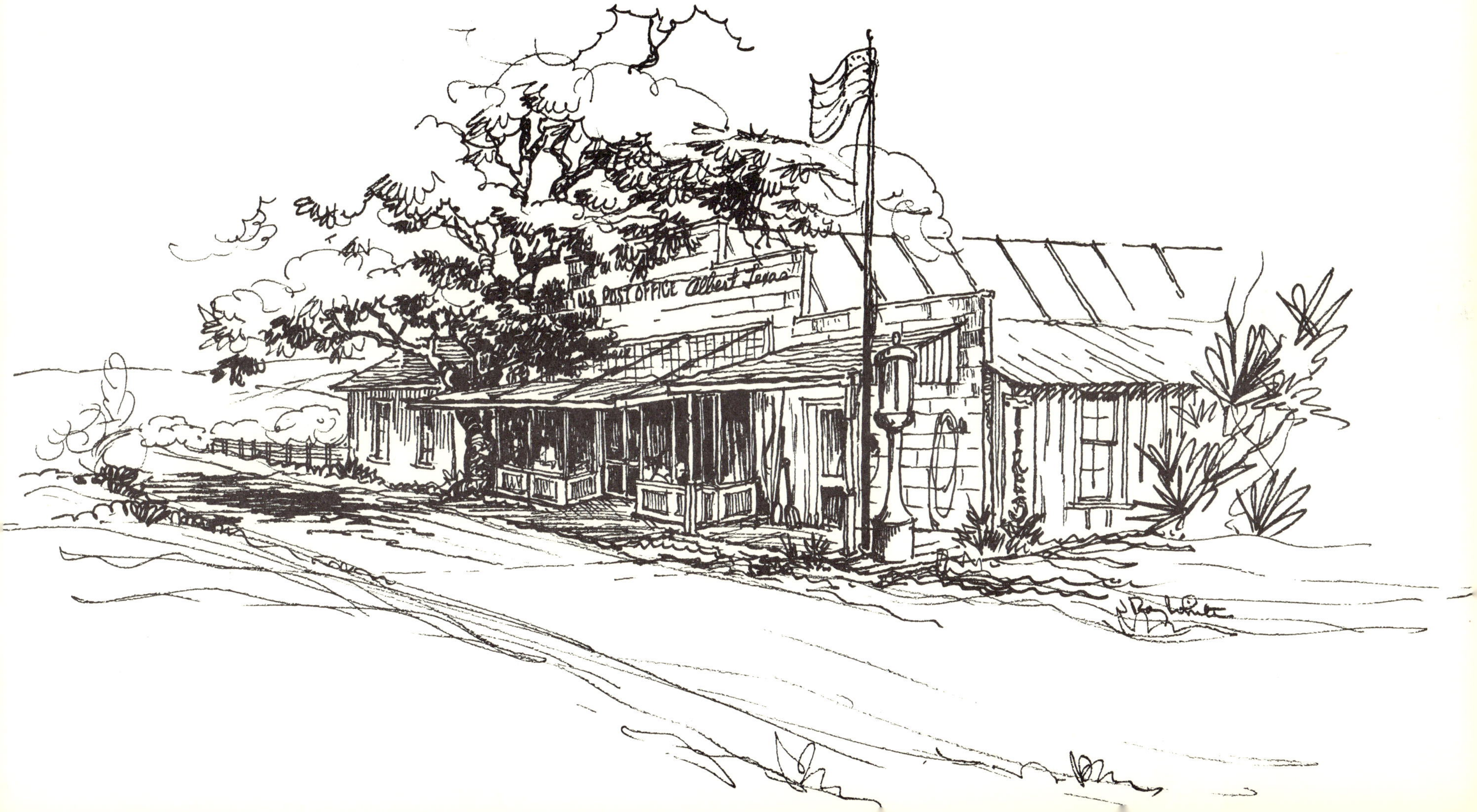
U.S. POST OFFICE Albert Texas

ALBERT SCHOOL

FOR SEVENTY YEARS the Albert School has been used to teach little boys and girls. Between times it has served as a community center. Elections have been held there, and are still held there. Here's where the Woodmen of the World hold their fraternal meetings, and here the farmers decide how to organize to improve their world, and here the socials are held. The community club still meets at the Albert Schoolhouse to play dominoes and "42." Here a young boy, not quite the usual starting age, had his first formal schooling. From the results it would seem to have been adequate.

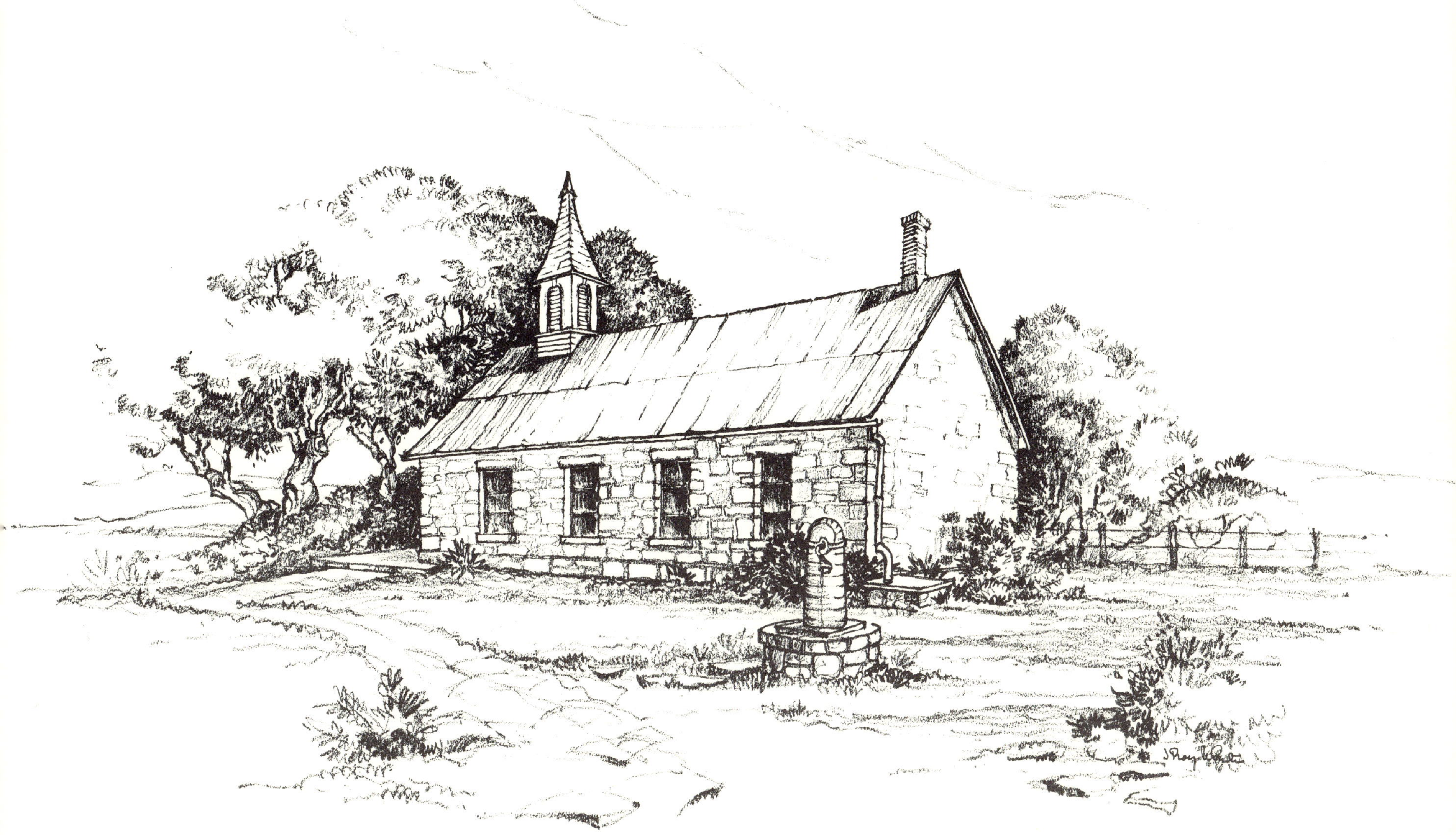

ALBERT ROAD LOG HOUSE
near Stonewall

ROBERT ARHELGER SR. borrowed eight hundred dollars to buy the hundred acres on which he built this house about 1882. For more than a third of a century he barely made a living and met his interest payments. When he sold the place in 1919, he still owed the eight hundred dollars principal. To Arhelger's credit is the fact that he tried every which way to make the land pay—cotton, orchards, and garden truck. The only real asset was a forty-five foot well with some of the coldest, freshest water in the region. But the land really wasn't worth the struggle, and now the house, unpainted and rotting, and the trees, leafless and stark, proclaim quietly what Arhelger could have told you after lasting thirty-seven years from youth's hopes to old age's tired despair.

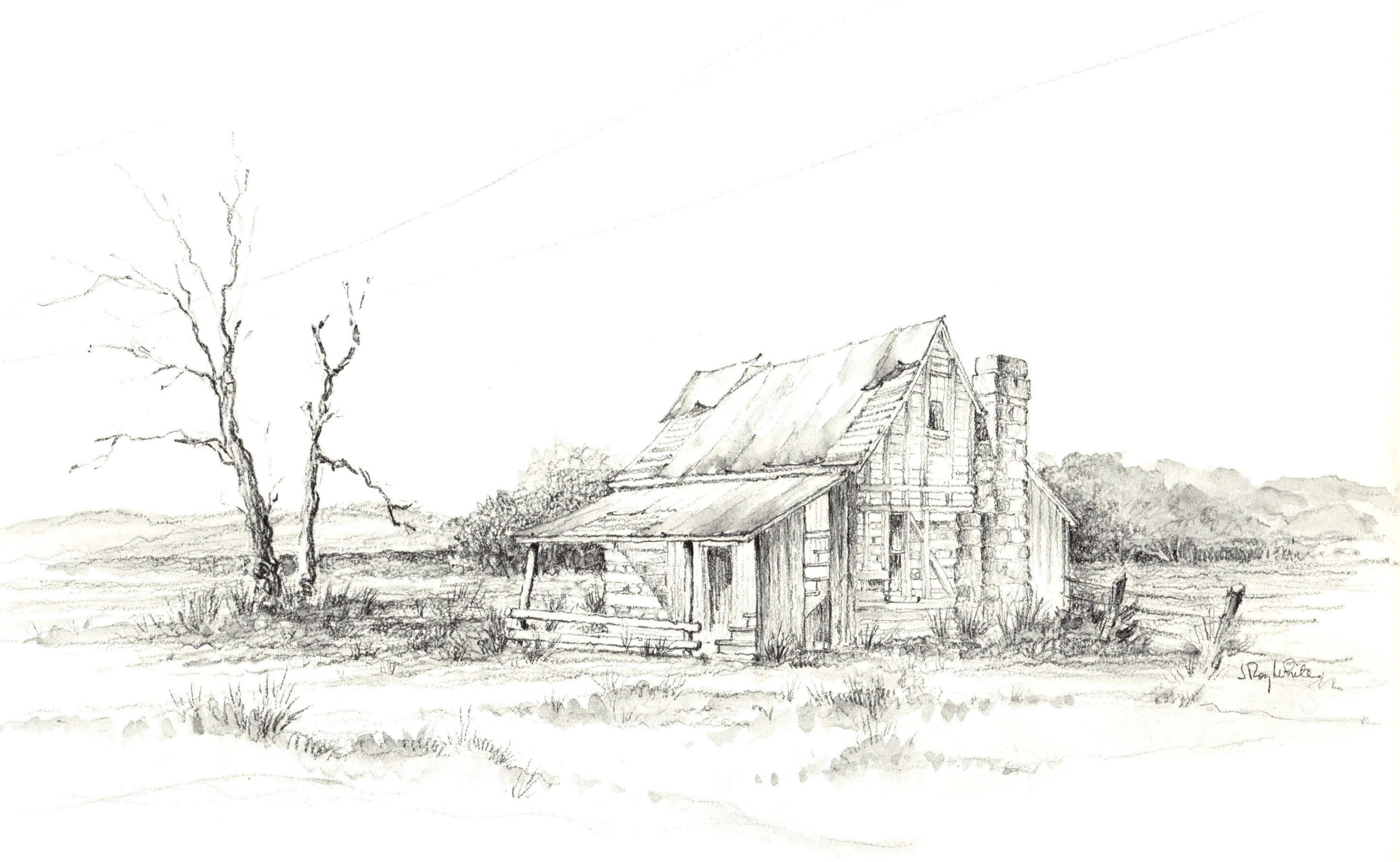
J Roy White

DANZ HOUSE
on Doublehorn Road

IF THE GOOD FAIRY gave me my choice of any house in the Hill Country, it would be this Danz house north of Stonewall. On a clear day, which is almost any day, you can sit on the front gallery and look southward into infinity. The wave of hills that lie south of Johnson City silhouette the low horizon. Somewhere down there is Stonewall and nearby is the LBJ Ranch complex, but they all look infinitesimal or do not seem to exist at all. The world largely consists of you and whoever is sitting on the gallery beside you. No sounds except the wonderful natural sounds. On the stillest day a breeze blows. On a windy day you dress to keep the wind away. A few pieces of rusted, wrecked machinery, here and there a strand of barbed wire that dangles, now and then a small flock of chickens, and that is all. The sky is clear, the sun brilliant in the day, and the stars as luminous at night, with no smoke, no dust, nothing man-made to interrupt. Here is solitude. Here man feels in spirit with the Infinite.

Presently owned by Jay Danz, this house was originally built by Henry Immel—the first two rooms about 1898, with Peter Nebgen as the mason. After Adolph Danz bought the house, he added two more rooms.

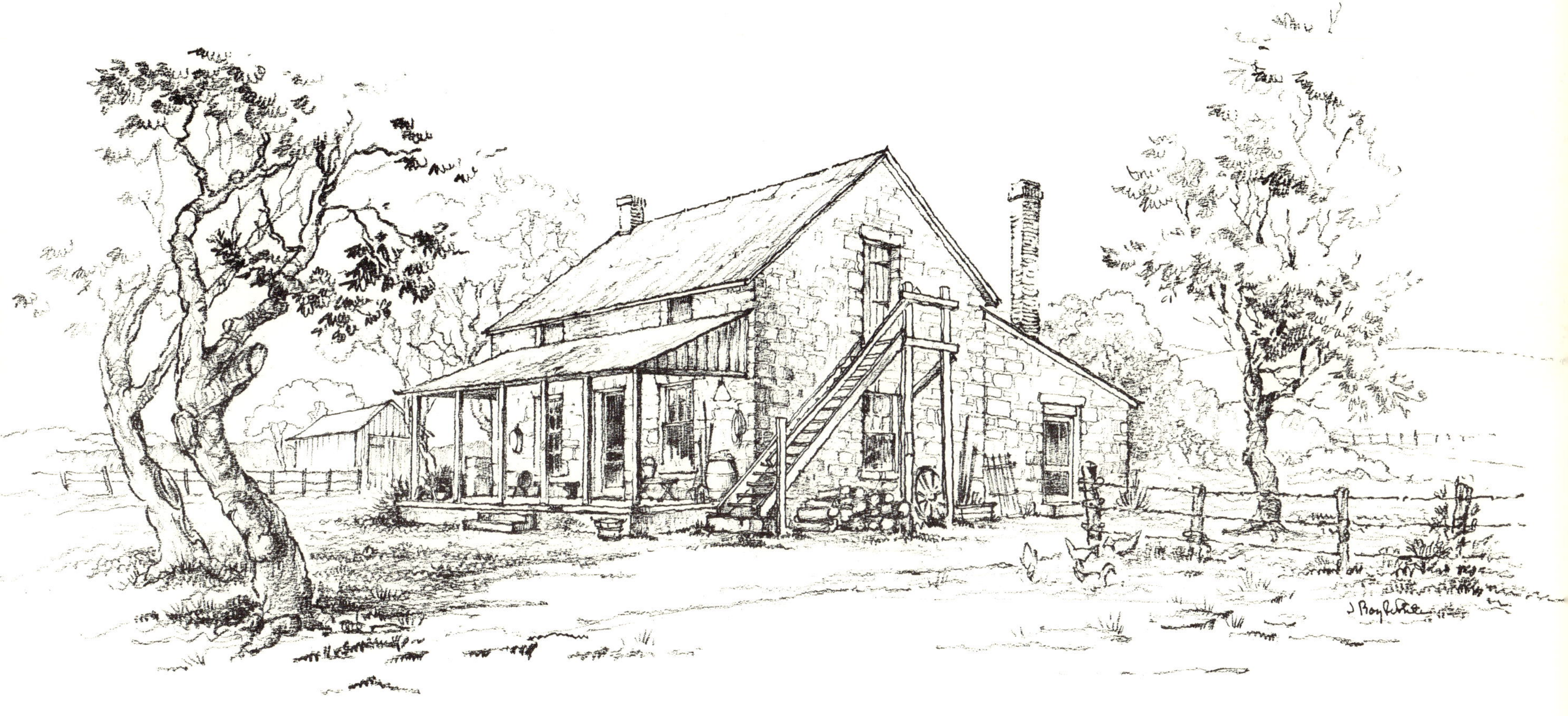

ALBERT NEBGEN HOME
Stonewall

THIS MAY BE a good place to tell about Joe Fr. Stahl, a native of Mademuehlen in Herzogtum von Nassau, who brought his wife and three children to Fredericksburg in the fall of 1852. Four years later he moved towards Stonewall to Cave Creek, took up a hundred and sixty acres of government land, built a log house, and with his family's aid cleared and cultivated fourteen acres of land with one yoke of oxen. In his fifth year on the new place Herr Stahl left one May morning to look for a cow and calf which he believed to be hiding out in the pasture. He took his noon lunch, a pocketknife, and a long whip. He told his wife he would be back when he had found the strays. He frequently left for several days when he was on a search. But when Wednesday came and her husband had not returned, Fraulein Stahl called in neighbors. In the afternoon fifteen men began a search. They searched for two days before they found his body at Rocky Branch three miles northeast of Stonewall. He lay face down with two arrows in his back and one in his neck, evidently shot from behind. He was naked except for his shoes, which were taken to his wife for identification. Joe Fr. Stahl had lived in the New World for only nine years, and was but forty when he died. With two surviving sons the widow cut and split thirty-five hundred fence rails to enclose the homestead. Cave Creek was a long way from the neighborliness and the security of Mademuehlen.

As for the house, it began as Ludwig's store, was in part torn down and in part added to, and had a period under William Hitzfeld as a post office.

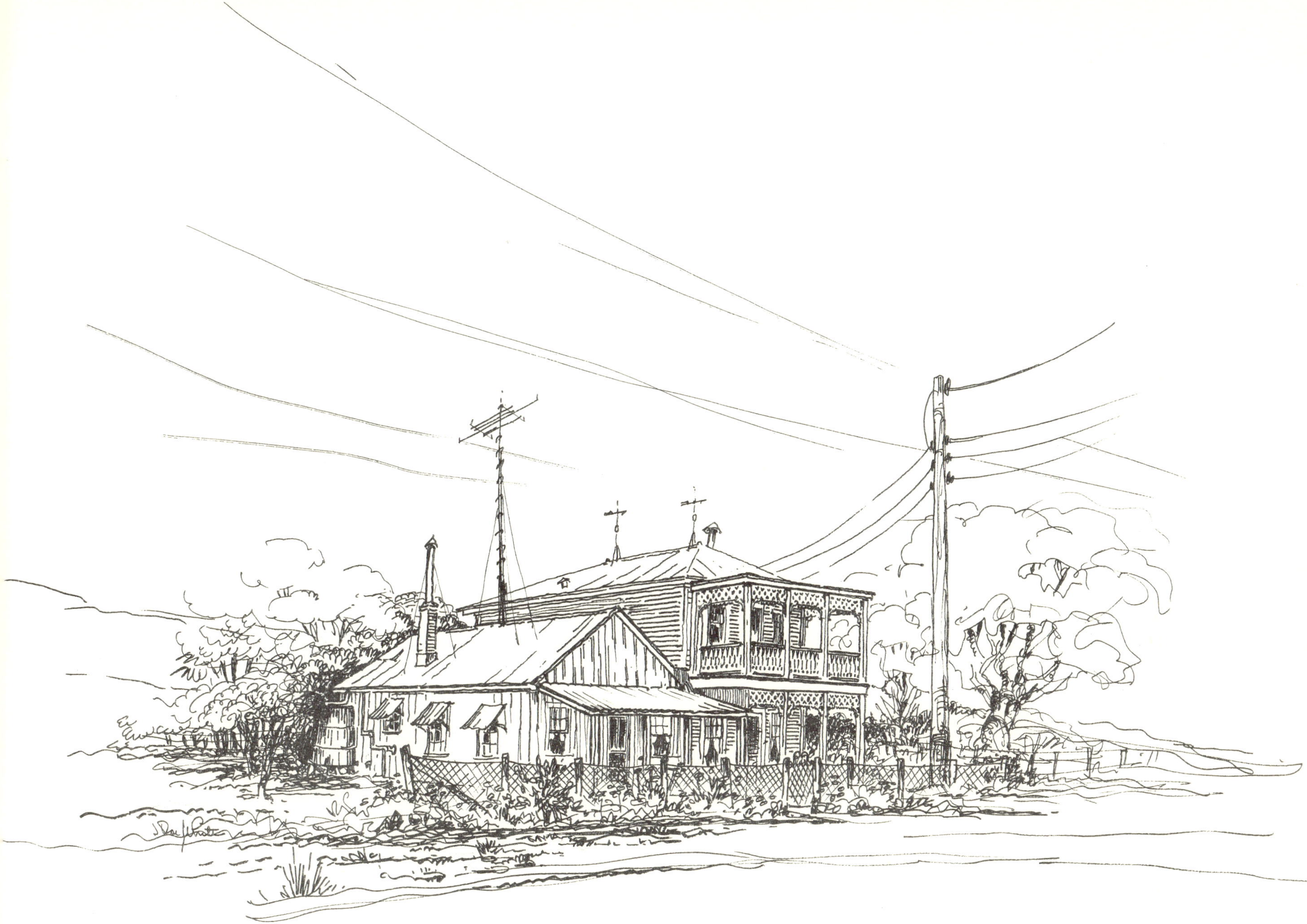

STONE HOUSE
Stonewall

WHEN HENRY JACOBY built this house more than three-quarters of a century ago on one hundred acres of unfenced, cleared farmland, Harry Hitzfeld remembers that the Pedernales froze solid and a recent immigrant from Denmark ice-skated on the river. On better days the neighbors would walk down to Burg's Store to visit and play cards. Bridge and poker are all right in their place, but for a real evening, try "Solo" and "High Five."

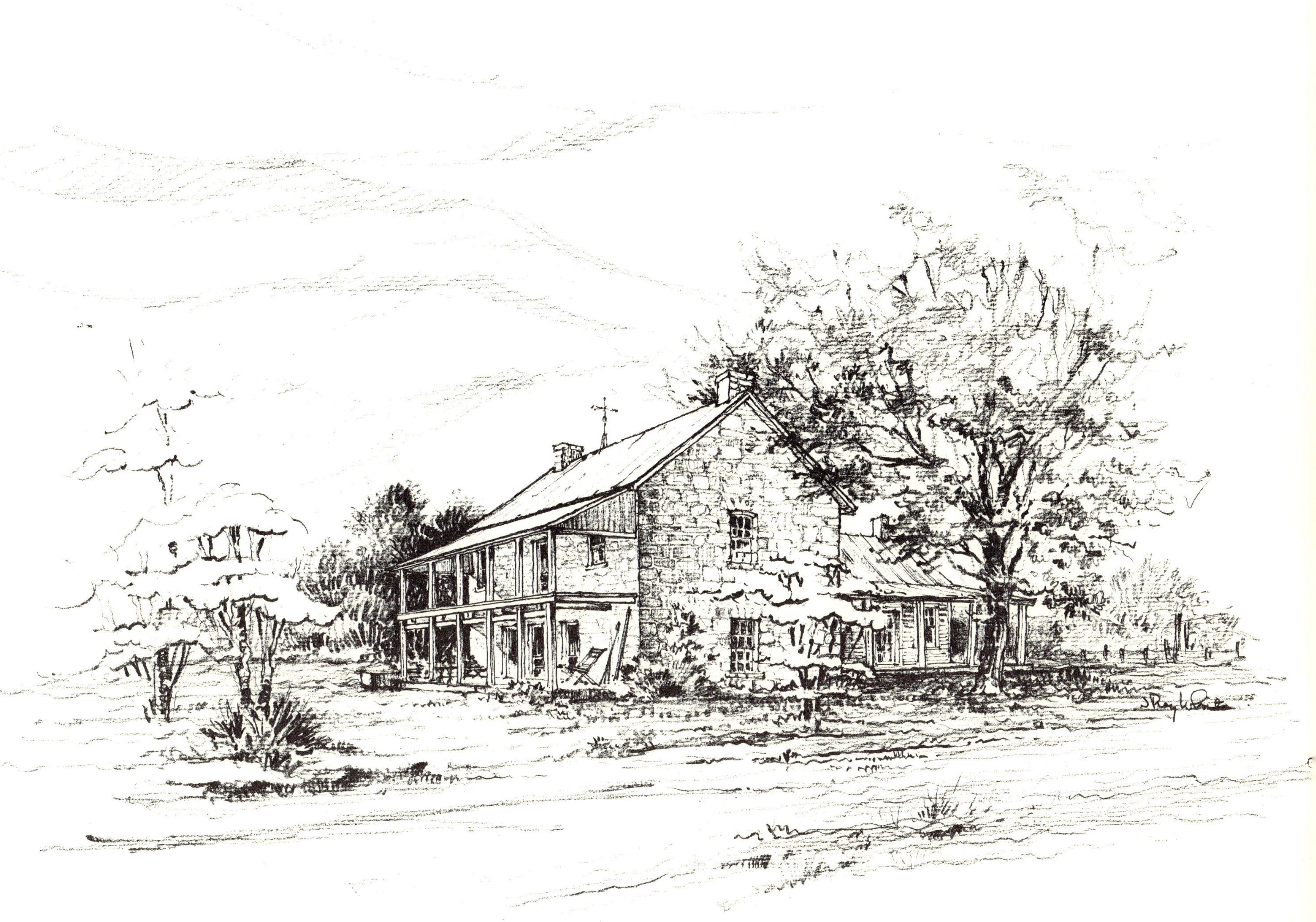

NUÑEZ HOUSE
near Stonewall

THE EARLY PEOPLE came into the Hill Country, like the mountain climbers, because it was there and because it was available. I. M. Nuñez, of Spanish-Jewish ancestry, bought thousands of acres south of the Pedernales at fifty cents an acre. He established a stage stop, laid out a town called Millville, and then asked that its post office be named for a general whom he had served in the Civil War, Stonewall Jackson. Major Nuñez did not get the full name honoring the general, but the first name couldn't have been more fortuitous.

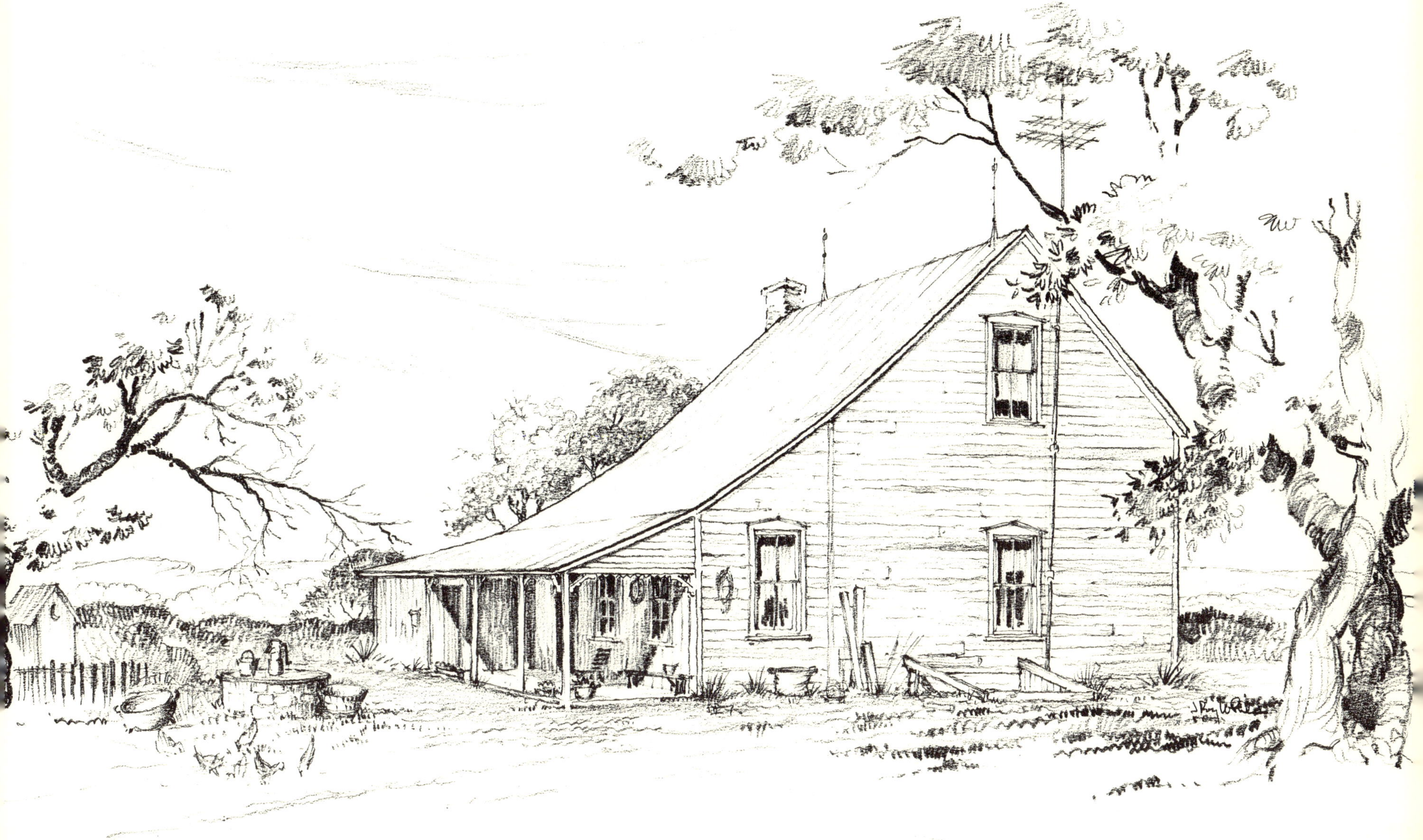

SISTERDALE SCHOOL

A SKETCHBOOK like this could go on and on. Down every country lane, beyond every gate, and across each cattleguard lies something from the past, something to be seen and savored. Even the names of the towns—Blanco, Stonewall, Comfort, Kendalia, Mountain Home, Twin Sisters, Round Mountain, Meusebach Creek, Rheingold, Boerne, Blumenthal, and Sisterdale. They are names worth pronouncing, and places worth remembering.

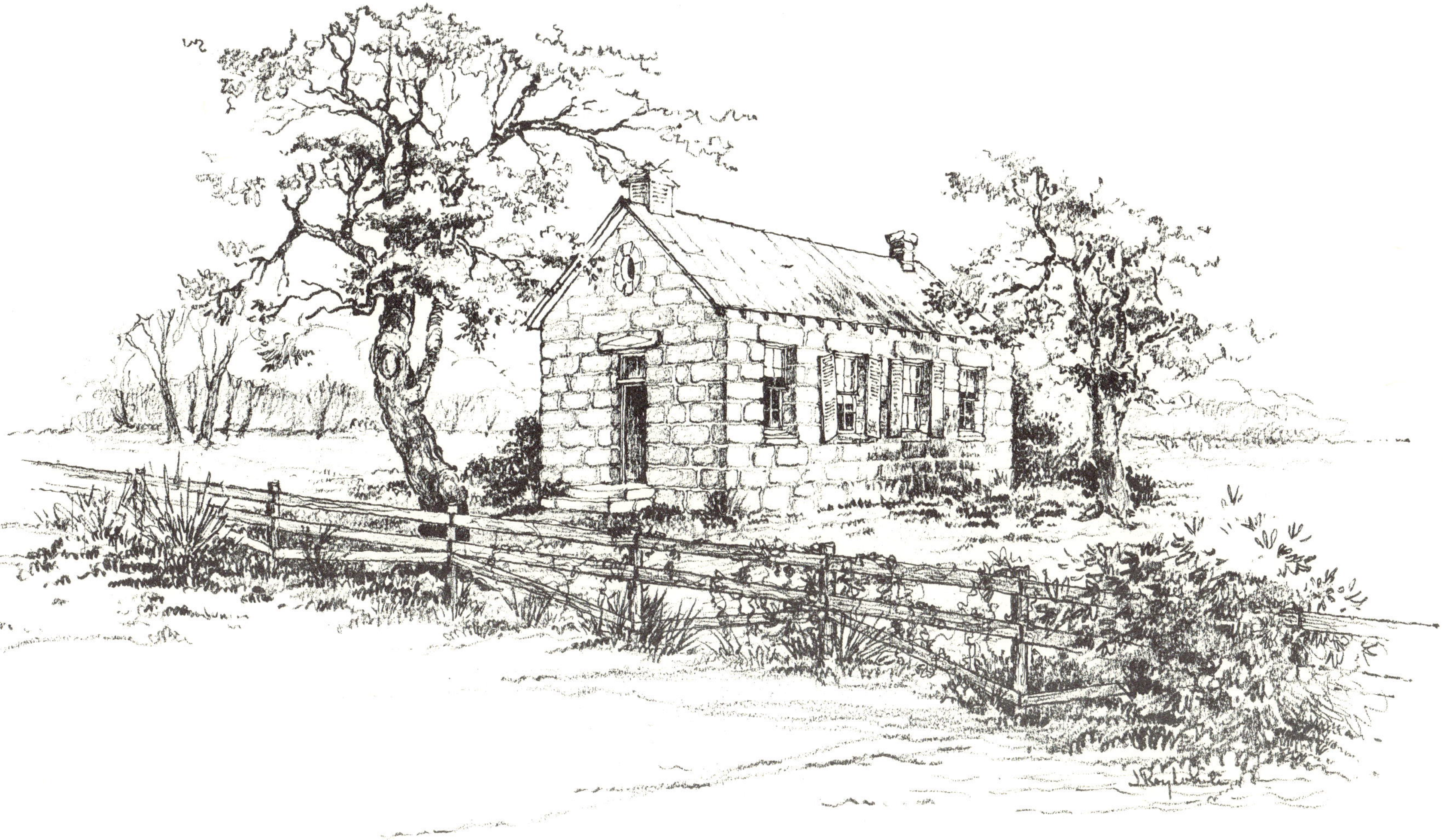

RUDY'S BARNS
near Sisterdale
56

THE GERMAN SMALL BARN resembles its builders—sturdy, upright, plain, and almost stark in its simplicity and its setting. Like its builders it had to be noticed, and it did what it was supposed to do.

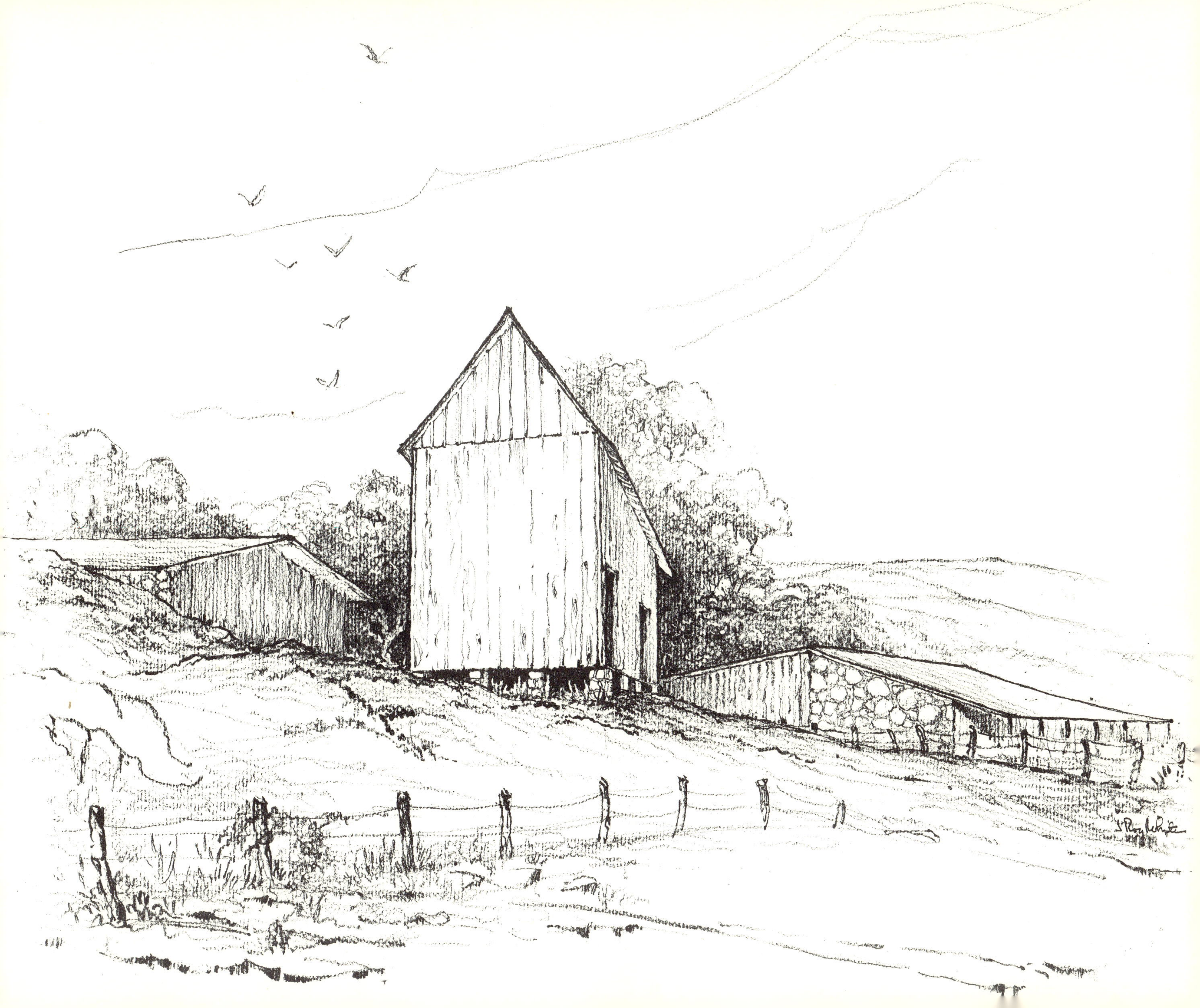

LUCKENBACH
POST OFFICE

AUGUST ENGEL traveled around on horseback as a circuit rider, dropping in to preach wherever he could get two people who would listen. That left his wife alone at home in the middle 1850's. Being an enterprising woman, Mrs. Engel started trading and bartering with the Indians. Hers was an idyllic spot, with a mott of live oak trees just across the road in one direction, while in another a small brook comes through a grassy wooded area. Along the brook is an abandoned cotton gin, with all its silent machinery and its old engine house with its boiler and tall smokestack reminding of a long-past era when men grew cotton here. It is a crossroads that invites you to stop to visit with Benno Engel, or to sit under the shade of one of the oak, pecan, or cypress trees to look at the Buster Brown and Lucky Strike signs, as well as the old hand-gasoline pump that stands outside the unpainted general store and post office. The "hills of God," some of the Germans call this land. They are speaking precisely.

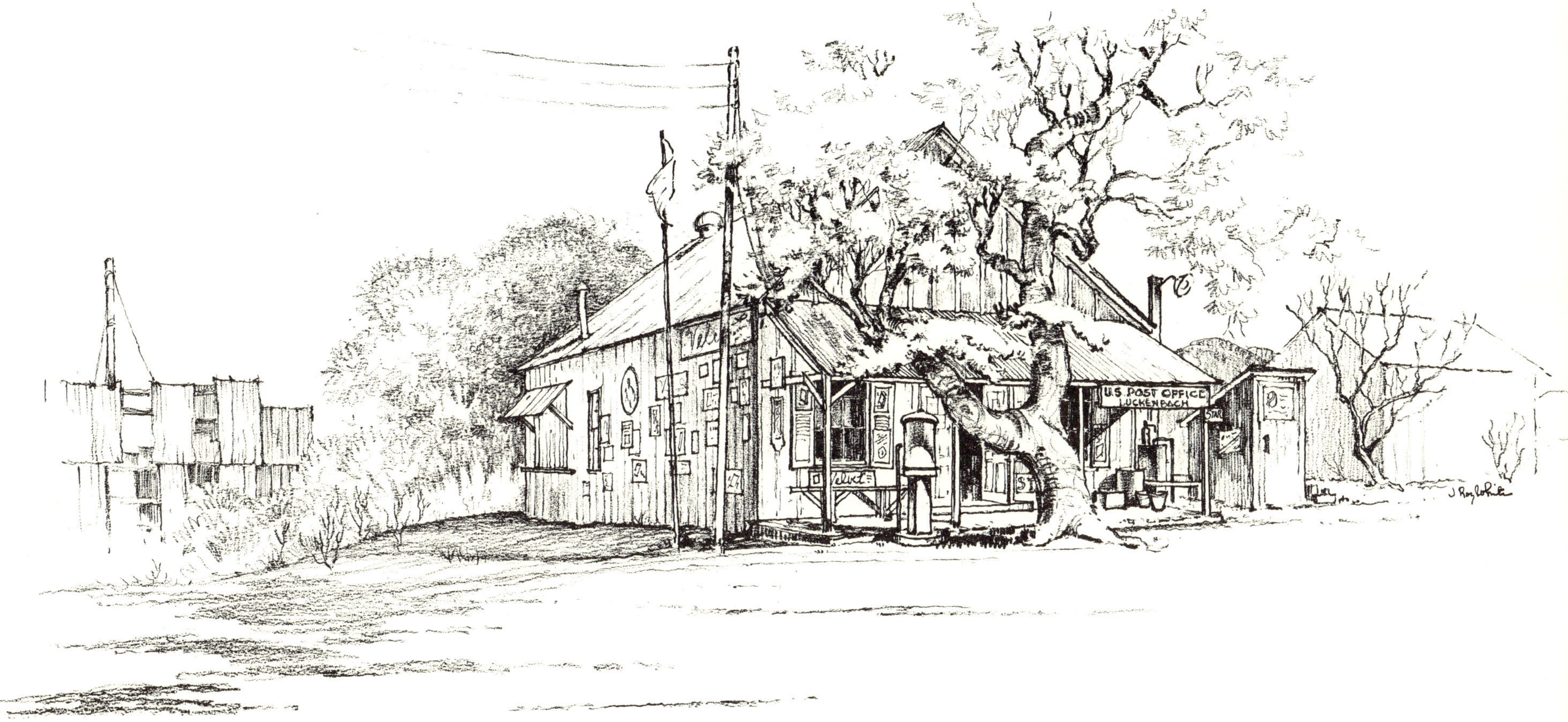
U.S. POST OFFICE
LUCKENBACH
STAR
J Roy White

BLUMENTHAL   THERE IS A CATTLE TRADITION in this country. Men to the east and men to the west and men to the south brought cattle through here when the land was unfenced and the good grass was all beyond the Indian Territory. Ab Blocker, whom J. Frank Dobie branded as the greatest of the trail drivers, worked the area. It was Ab Blocker who suggested the brand XIT to Barbecue Campbell. And Samuel Ealy Johnson Sr. along with his brother, J. T. Johnson, took cattle up the trails to far-off Kansas, and later even farther to Wyoming and Montana. Men like these came back to places like Hugo Shefer's store and saloon in Blumenthal to tell just how broad and alien the world really was.

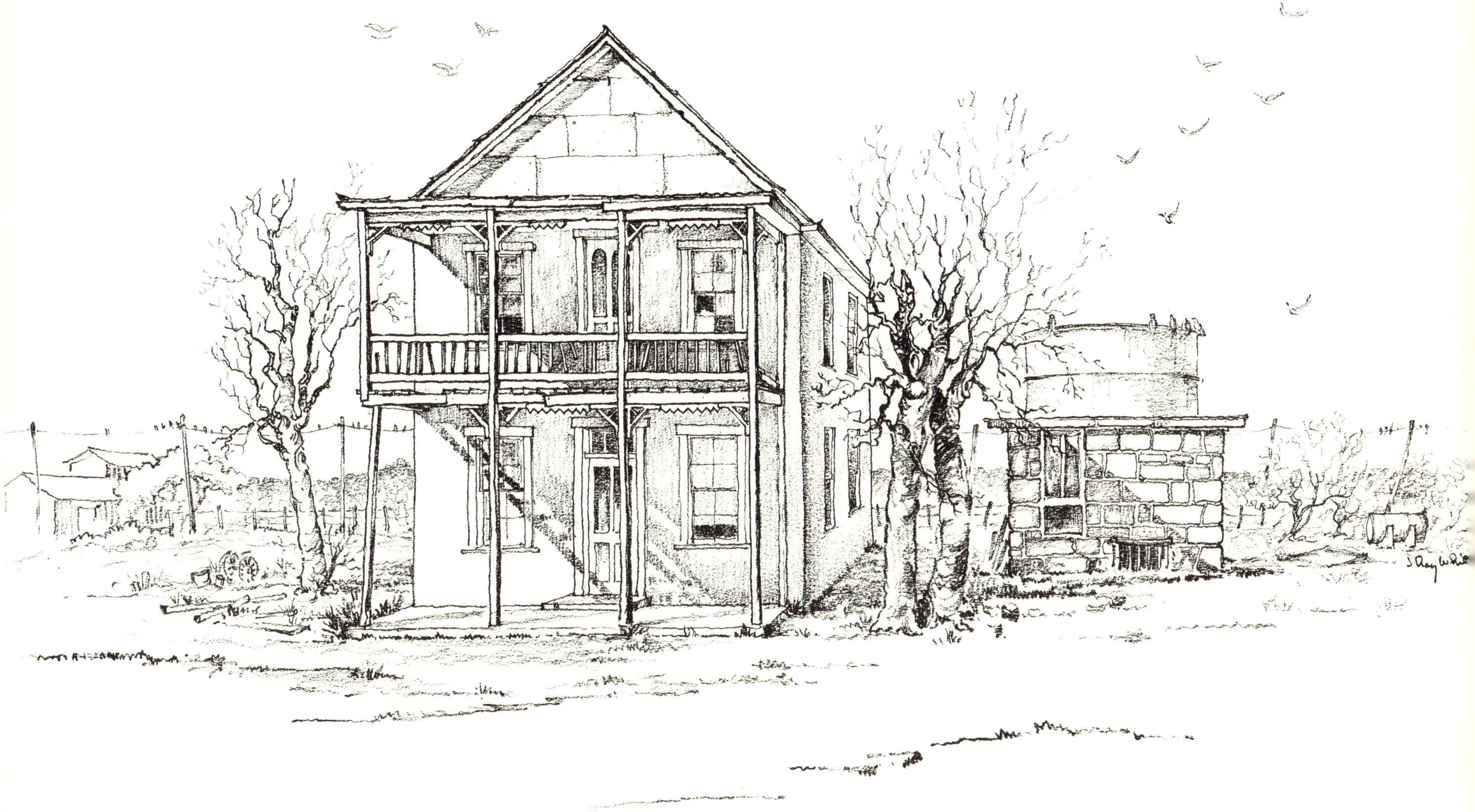

FARMHOUSE
near Blumenthal

GOOD HOUSES and good neighbors make a good region. But these qualities cannot be seen readily by the outsider. What makes the Hill Country worth preserving and experiencing is its unexpected vistas of log cabins and limestone houses and outbuildings. They evoke a past which in this changing world has resisted change. The Hill Country gives us an opportunity to see life as it was—still being lived right now.

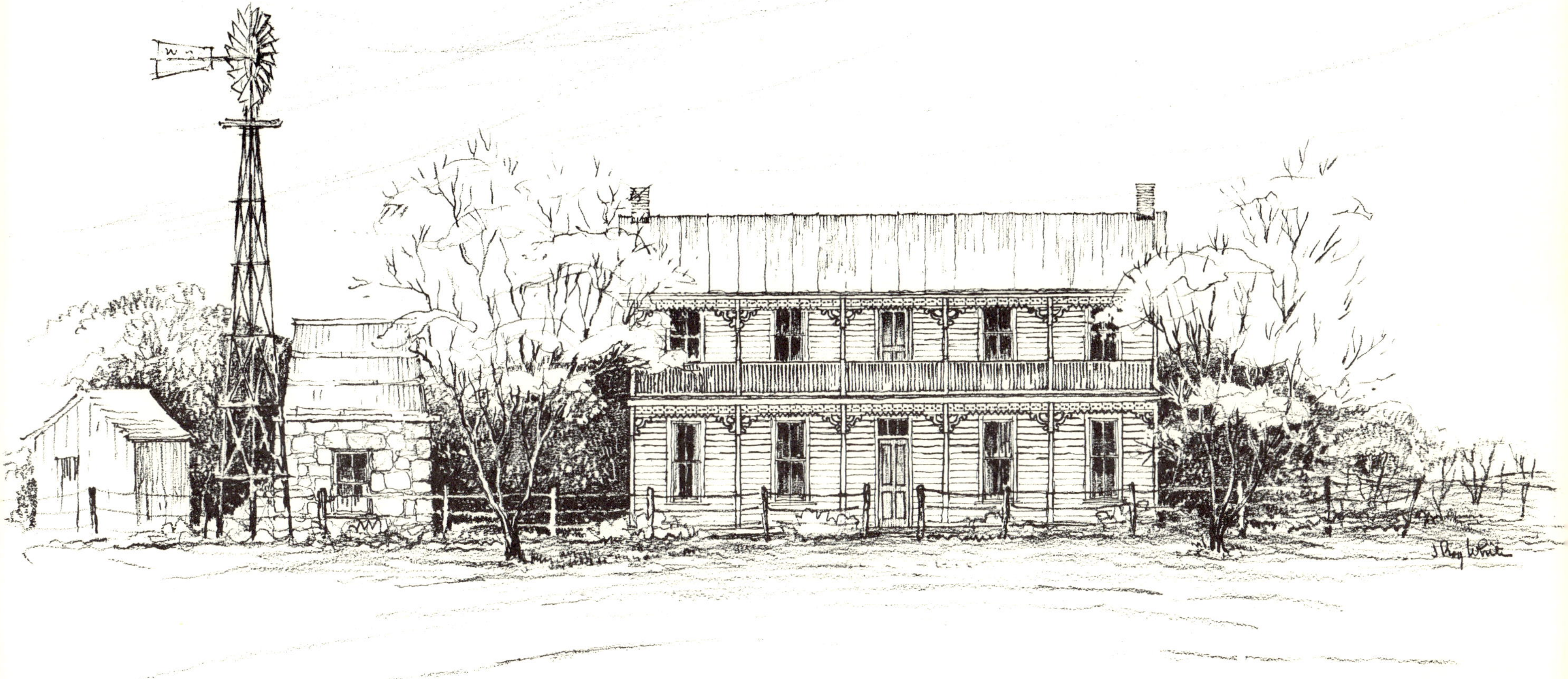

FREDERICKSBURG FACHVERK HOUSE

FREDERICKSBURG is a small treasure trove of the Germanic construction known as *fachverk*. Whereas most houses in these early days were built with perpendicular and horizontal strains, many Germans went back to a crisscrossing system that intrigues even now. One disintegrating Fredericksburg house has lost most of its sides, so that the *fachverk* shows like the insides of those plastic automobiles one sees at state fairs. This particular house has been deserted so long that huge grapevines and old stumps of trees have sprouted and entwined about the perpendicular timbers, and in some cases have competed those logs right out of existence.

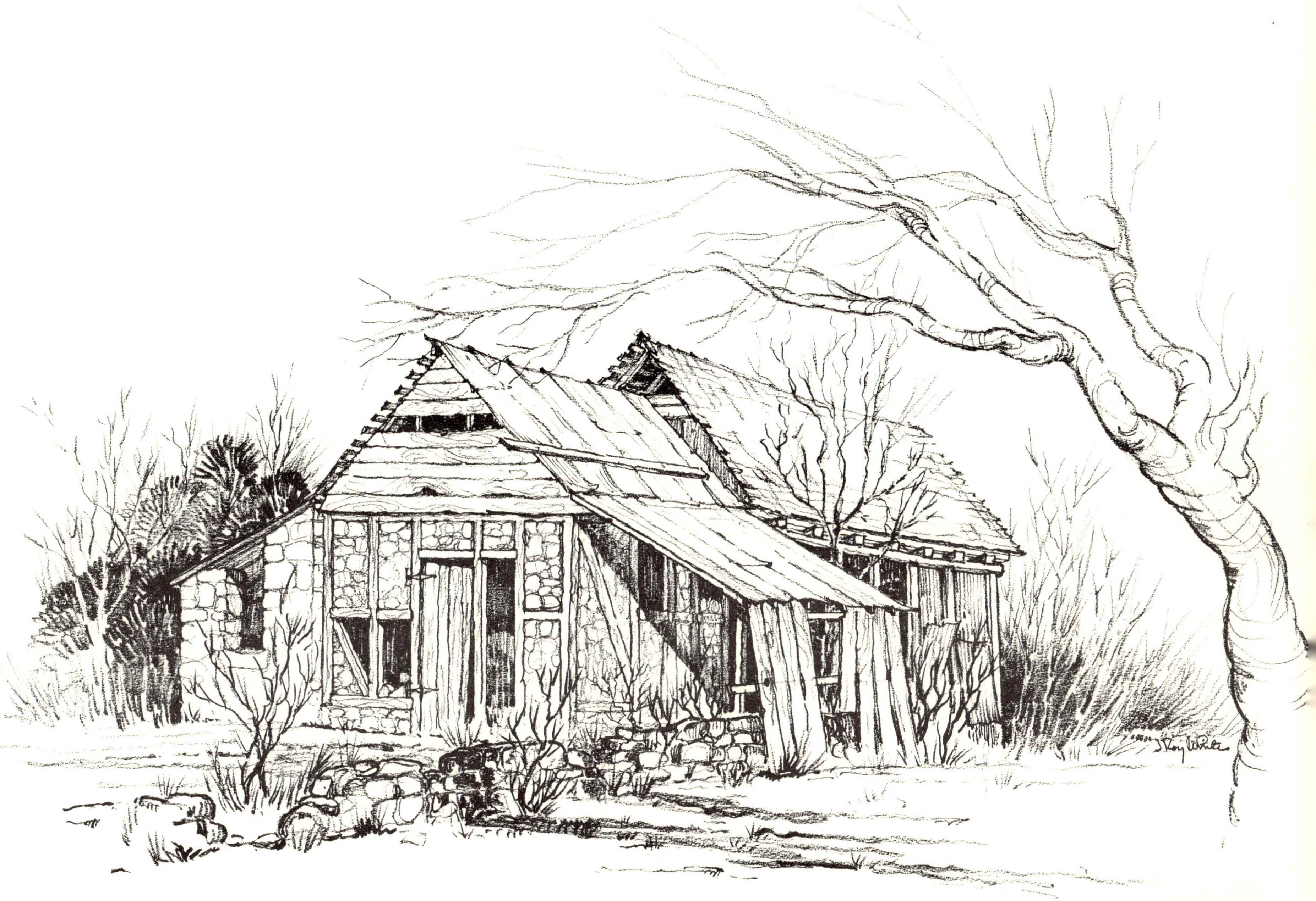
J Roy White

FREDERICKSBURG SHOP

FREDERICKSBURG is on its way to becoming a kind of Teutonic Texas version of Colonial Williamsburg. Nothing so grandiose, genteel, or expensive. But the people there have caught the spirit. They are not only preserving the considerable that is left, but on their own, without help from foundations or government agencies or commissions or anything else, are keeping a tight rein on new construction. Fredericksburg is a small museum in itself, a rare jewel, still a bit unpolished, that is waiting to be discovered.

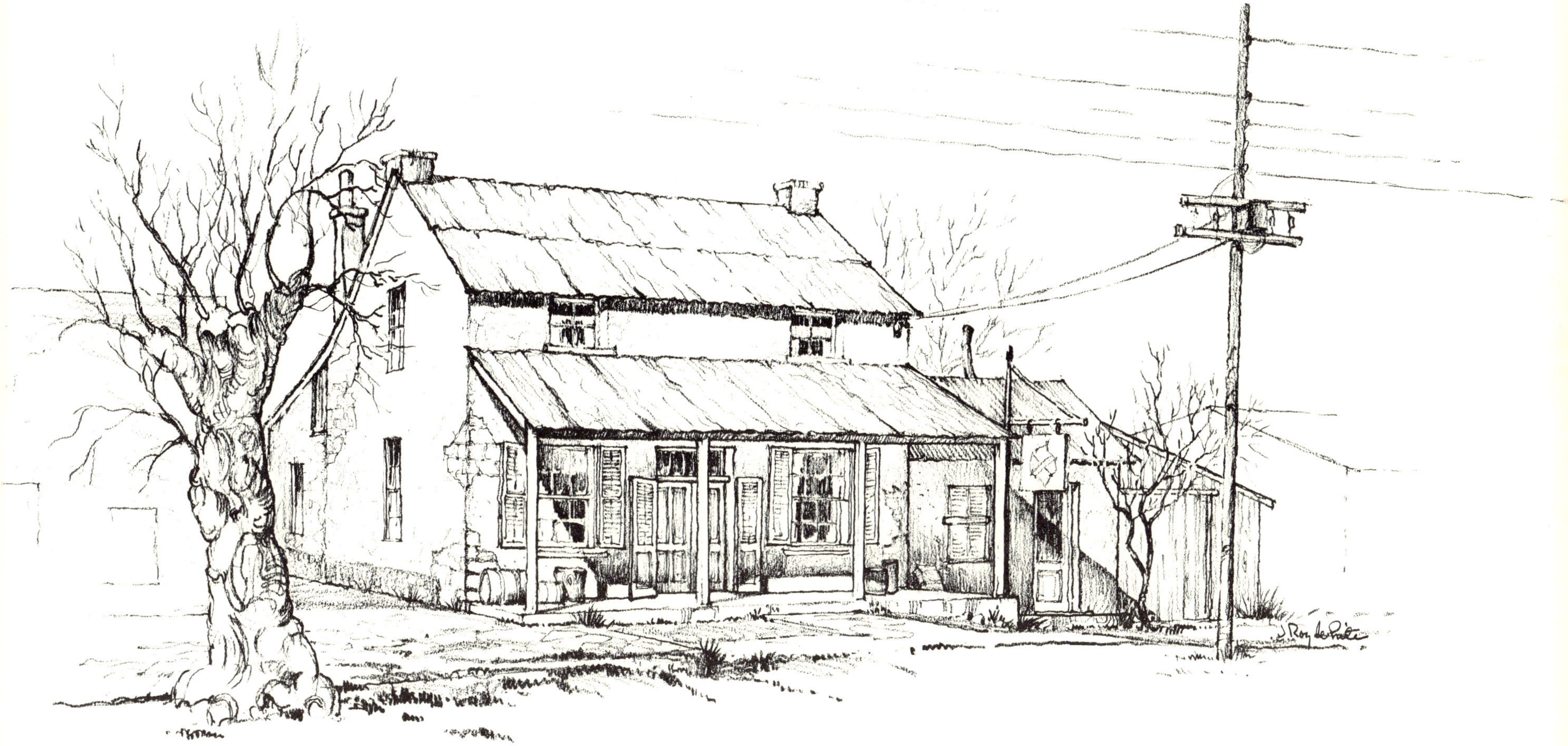

FREDERICKSBURG
SUNDAY HOUSE
A.D. 1968

IN THE DAYS of slow travel the German farmers would bring their families into Fredericksburg, along with their wagonloads of what they had managed to grow, trap, or kill. Because they could not go and return in one day, they built little Sunday houses, many of which still stand, as a place to spend the weekend. While they were there, they could not only trade and visit, but also attend the House of the Lord. To a modern world which flees to a cabin in the mountains or at the seashore on weekends, this was civilization in reverse.

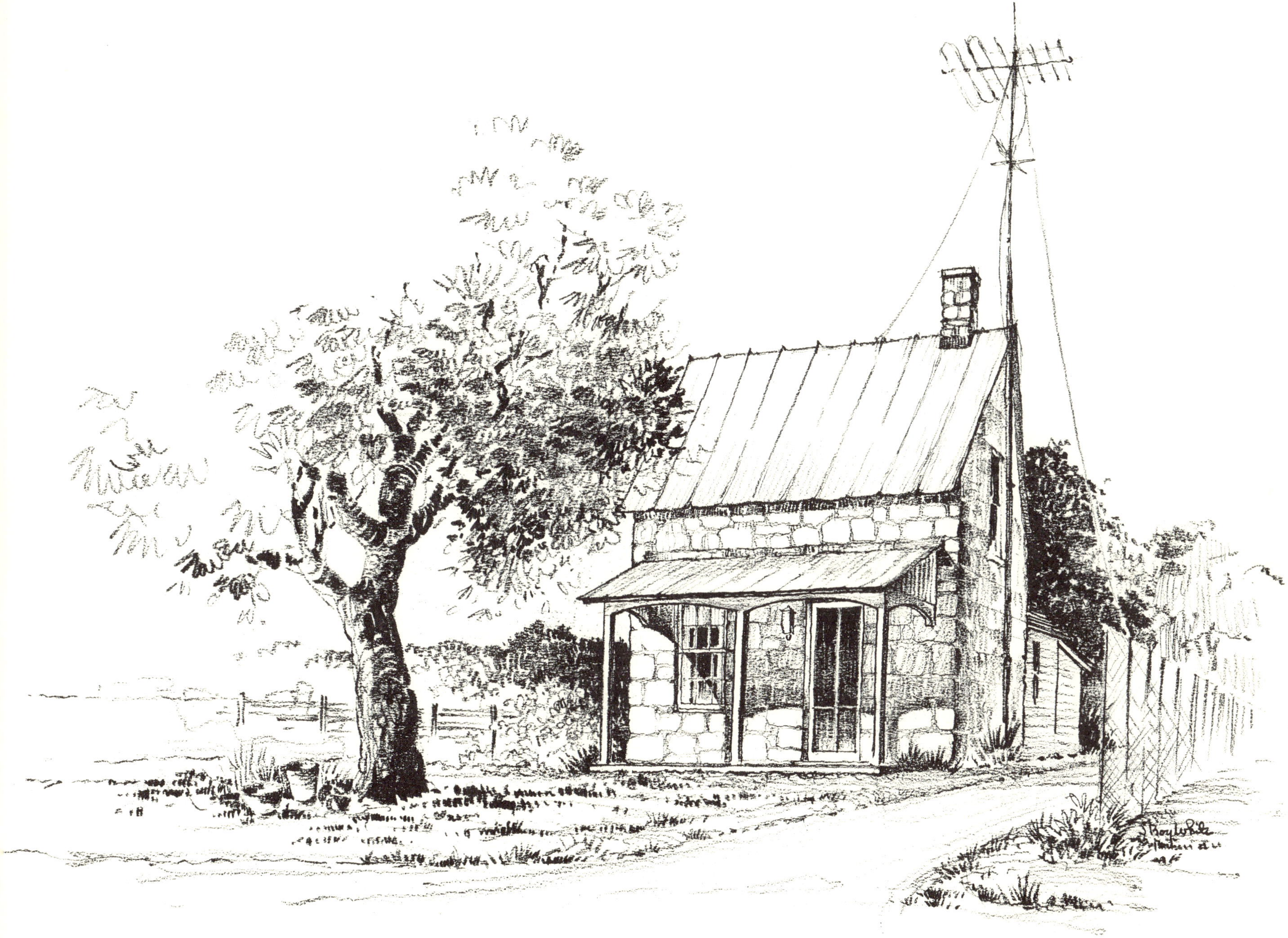

AFTERWORD

WHEN ONE OF THE SULTEMEIERS saw the old home place sketch he wondered how anyone knew to put the front gate "where it used to be". Nobody asked—the landscape was just revised to fit the picture. Which is what has happened in many of the drawings: trees have been removed, wells dug and fences built and at least one outhouse brought into view from behind the bushes. If some places don't look quite the same it's all for an attempt at better composition and interest.

Other than to satisfy some notions of what a picture should look like, a "revised landscape" shouldn't actually be necessary, because the first settlers in the hill country seemed to have a certain knack for locating their homes to take advantage of the good summer breezes and to protect themselves from the bad winter freezes. They usually had a view of the countryside and when at all possible found a place near a stream and sheltered by trees. When they got as close as they could to such an ideal site they went ahead and put up a log cabin. The materials were at hand and that's the way the folks back home had done it. Hill country oaks make picturesque trees but they leave something to be desired for log cabins. Frame houses aplenty hide old log cabins forgotten or unknown by present owners and covered over with time and with boards or wood siding or pressed tin or stucco or rocks—or anything to keep out the rain.

The "fachverk" houses of Fredericksburg were a little more successful. They recaptured a bit of the brick and half-timber work in the old country, but brick was not available and stonework had to be used to fill in the spaces between the hand-hewn timbers. Rain was a problem for "fachverk" as well as log construction. In later times stone houses and barns were quite substantial and have spent the years well in coloring and softening their beautiful stonework textures.

When milled lumber and stock millwork became available in the nineties, most houses were built of wood with lots of robust Victorian gingerbread more in keeping with Victoria's German ancestry than was the English variety. Many of the farmhouses of this period are excellently proportioned and detailed. The farmhouse near Blumenthal just north of the highway is a good example.

Why did I do these sketches? Maybe because I think the old buildings deserve a sort of respect and attention, this being all I can give. Anyway, here they are. And they each seem to beg for just a little compassion, just a little understanding, from all of us—proud and happy when cared for, rugged and brave in their slow neglect and isolation.

JRW

Austin, Texas
September, 1968

Design by WILLIAM D. WITTLIFF